Defoe Abbott Marx Hardy Melville Montaigne Machiavelli Haggard Chesterton Cooper Emerson Joyce Austen Hugo Eliot Grimm

Stoker Carroll Christie Maupassant Byron Molière Schiller

Wilde Garnett Einstein Fitzgerald Engels Hawthorne Smith Kafka

Goethe Henry Kipling Doyle Hall

Baum Leslie Dumas Flaubert Turgenev Nietzsche Balzac Willis

Stockton Vatsyayana Crane

Burroughs Verne

Curtis Tocqueville Whitman Gogol Vinci

Homer Widger Tolstoy Busch

Darwin Thoreau Twain Scott

Potter Freud Zola Lawrence Plato Harte

Kant Jowett Stevenson Dickens Burton Hesse

Andersen

London Descartes Cervantes Voltaire Cooke

Poe Aristotle Wells

Hale James Hastings

Bunner Shakespeare Irving

Richter Chekhov Chambers

Doré Dante Swift da Shaw Wodehouse Benedict Alcott Pushkin

Newton

 tredition®

tredition was established in 2006 by Sandra Latusseck and Soenke Schulz. Based in Hamburg, Germany, tredition offers publishing solutions to authors and publishing houses, combined with world-wide distribution of printed and digital book content. tredition is uniquely positioned to enable authors and publishing houses to create books on their own terms and without conventional manu-facturing risks.

For more information please visit: www.tredition.com

TREDITION CLASSICS

This book is part of the TREDITION CLASSICS series. The creators of this series are united by passion for literature and driven by the intention of making all public domain books available in printed format again - worldwide. Most TREDITION CLASSICS titles have been out of print and off the bookstore shelves for decades. At tredition we believe that a great book never goes out of style and that its value is eternal. Several mostly non-profit literature projects provide content to tredition. To support their good work, tredition donates a portion of the proceeds from each sold copy. As a reader of a TREDITION CLASSICS book, you support our mission to save many of the amazing works of world literature from oblivion. See all available books at www.tredition.com.

Project Gutenberg

The content for this book has been graciously provided by Project Gutenberg. Project Gutenberg is a non-profit organization founded by Michael Hart in 1971 at the University of Illinois. The mission of Project Gutenberg is simple: To encourage the creation and distribu-tion of eBooks. Project Gutenberg is the first and largest collection of public domain eBooks.

New Ideals in Rural Schools

George Herbert Betts

Imprint

This book is part of TREDITION CLASSICS

Author: George Herbert Betts
Cover design: Buchgut, Berlin – Germany

Publisher: tredition GmbH, Hamburg - Germany
ISBN: 978-3-8472-2986-5

www.tredition.com
www.tredition.de

Riverside Educational Monographs

EDITED BY HENRY SUZZALLO

PROFESSOR OF THE PHILOSOPHY OF EDUCATION
TEACHERS COLLEGE, COLUMBIA UNIVERSITY

NEW IDEALS IN RURAL SCHOOLS

BY

GEORGE HERBERT BETTS, Ph.D.

PROFESSOR OF PSYCHOLOGY
CORNELL COLLEGE, IOWA

CONTENTS

EDITOR'S INTRODUCTION

In presenting a second monograph on the rural school problem in this series we register our sense of the importance of rural education. Too long have the rural schools suffered from neglect. Both the local communities and the State have overlooked the needs of the rural school system. At the present hour there is an earnest awakening of interest in rural life and its institutions. Already there is a small but certain movement of people toward the country and the vocation of agriculture. A period of agricultural prosperity, the reaction of men and women against the artificialities of city life, the development of farming through the application of science, and numerous other factors have made country life more congenial and have focused attention upon its further needs. It is natural, therefore, that the rural school should receive an increased share of attention.

Educational administrators, legislators, and publicists have become aware of their responsibility to provide the financial support and the efficient organization that is needed to develop [Pg vi] country schools. The more progressive of them are striving earnestly to provide laws that will aid rather than hamper the rural school system. In his monograph on *The Improvement of the Rural School*, Professor Cubberley has done much to interpret current efforts of this type. From the standpoint of state administration he has contributed much definite information and constructive suggestion as to how the State shall respond to the fundamental need for (1) more money, (2) better organization, and (3) real supervision for rural schools.

It is not so clear, however, that rural patrons, school directors, and teachers have become fully aware of their duty in the matter of rural school improvement. To be sure much has been done by way of experiment in many rural communities; but it can scarcely be said that rural communities in general are thoroughly awake to the importance of their schools. The evidence to the contrary is cumulative. The first immediate need is to reawaken interest in the school as a center of rural life, and to suggest ways and means of transmuting this communal interest into effective institutional methods. To this end, Professor Betts has been asked to treat the rural school problem from a standpoint somewhat different [Pg vii] from that assumed by Professor Cubberley; that is, from the point of view of the local community immediately related to, and concerned with, the rural school. In consequence his presentation emphasizes the things that ought to be done by the local authorities,—parent, trustee, and teacher. Its soundness may well be judged by the pertinent order of his discussion. Having stated his problem, he initiates his discussion by suggesting how the social relations of the school are to be reorganized; only later does he pass to the detail of curricula and teaching methods. It is a clear recognition of the fact that the community is the crucial factor in the making of a school. The State by sound fiscal and legislative policies may do much to make possible a better country school; but only the local authorities can realize it. The trained teacher with modern notions of efficiency may attempt to enlarge the curriculum and to employ newer methods of teaching, but his talents are useless if he is hampered by a conservative, unappreciative, and indifferent community. When the school becomes a social center of the community's interest and life, there will be no difficulty in achieving any policy which the State permits or which a skilled teacher urges. Scattered schools [Pg viii] will be consolidated, and isolated ungraded schools will be improved. Given an interested community, the modern teacher can vitalize every feature of the school, changing the formal curriculum into an interesting and liberalizing interpretation of country life and the pedantic drills and tasks of instruction into a skillful ministry to real and abiding human wants.

PREFACE

No rural population has yet been able permanently to maintain itself against the lure of the town or the city. Each civilization at one stage of its development comprises a large proportion of rural people. But the urban movement soon begins, and continues until all are living in villages, towns, and cities. Such has been the movement of population in all the older countries of high industrial development, as England, France, and Germany. A similar movement is at present going on rapidly in the United States.

No great social movement ever comes by chance; it is always to be explained by deep-seated and adequate causes. The causes lying back of the rapid growth of our cities at the expense of our rural districts are very far from simple. They involve a great complex of social, educational, and economic forces. As the spirit of adventure and pioneering finds less to stimulate it, the gregarious impulse, the tendency to flock together for our work and our play, gains in ascendancy. Growing out of the greater intellectual opportunities and demands of modern [Pg x] times, the standard of education has greatly advanced. And under the incentive of present-day economic success and luxury, comfortable circumstances and a moderate competence no longer satisfy our people. Hence they turn to the city, looking to find there the coveted social, educational, or economic opportunities.

It is doubtful, therefore, whether, even with improved conditions of country life, the urbanization of our rural people can be wholly checked. But it can be greatly retarded if the right agencies are set at work. The rural school should be made and can be made one of the most important of these agencies, although at the present time its influence is chiefly negative. With the hope of offering some help, however slight, in adjusting the rural school to its problem, this little volume is written by one who himself belongs to the rural community by birth and early education and occupation.

G. H. B.

Cornell College, *February*, 1913.

NEW IDEALS IN RURAL SCHOOLS

I

THE RURAL SCHOOL AND ITS PROBLEM

[Pg 1]

The general problem of the rural school

The general problem of the rural school is the same as that of any other type of school—to render to the community the largest possible returns upon its investment in education with the least possible waste. Schools are great education factories set up at public expense. The raw material consists of the children of succeeding generations, helpless and inefficient because of ignorance and immaturity. The school is to turn out as its product men and women ready and able to take up their part in the great world of activities going on about them. It is in this way, in efficient education, that society gets its return for its investment in the schools.

The word "education" has in recent years been taking on a new and more vital meaning. In earlier times the value of education was as [Pg 2] sumed, or vaguely taken on faith. Education was supposed to consist of so much "learning," or a given amount of "discipline," or a certain quantity of "culture." Under the newer definition, education may include all these things, but it must do more; it *must relate itself immediately and concretely to the business of living*. We no longer inquire of one how much he knows, or the degree to which his powers have been "cultivated"; but rather to what extent his education has led to a more fruitful life in the home, the state, the church, and other social institutions; how largely it has helped him to more effective work in a worthy occupation; and whether it has resulted in greater enjoyment and appreciation of the finer values of personal experience,—in short, whether for him education spells *efficiency*.

We are thus coming to see that education must enable the individual to meet the real problems of actual experience as they are confronted in the day's life. Nor can the help rendered be indefinite, intangible, or in any degree uncertain. It must definitely adjust one to his place, and cause him to grow in it, accomplishing the most for himself and for society; it must add to the largeness of his personal life, and at the same time increase his working efficiency. [Pg 3]

This is to say that one's education must (1) furnish him with the particular *knowledge* required for the life that he is to live, whether it be in the shop, on the farm, or in the profession. For knowledge lies at the basis of all efficiency and success in whatever occupation. Education must (2) shape the *attitude*, so that the individual will confront his part of the world's work or its play in the right spirit. It must not leave him a parasite, whether from wealth or from poverty, ready to prey upon others; but must make him willing and glad to do his share. Education must (3) also give the individual training in *technique*, or the skill required in his different activities; not to do this is at best but to leave him a well-informed and well-intentioned bungler, falling far short of efficiency.

The great function of the school, therefore, is to supply the means by which the requisite *knowledge, attitude*, and *skill* can be developed. It is true that the child does not depend on the school alone for his knowledge, his attitude, and his skill. For the school is only one of many influences operating on his life. Much of the most vital knowledge is not taught in the school but picked up outside; a great part of the child's attitude toward life is formed through the rela [Pg 4] tions of the home, the community, and the various other points of contact with society; and much of his skill in doing is developed in a thousand ways without being taught. Yet the fact remains that the school is organized and supported by society to make sure about these things, to see that the child does not lack in knowledge, attitude, or skill. They must not be left to chance; where the educative influences outside the school have not been sufficient, the school must take hold. Its part is to supplement and organize with conscious purpose what the other agencies have accomplished in the education of the child. The ultimate purpose of the school is *to make certain of efficiency*.

The means by which the school is to accomplish these ends are (1) the *social organization* of the school, or the life and activities that go on in the school from day to day; (2) the *curriculum,* or the subject-matter which the child is given to master; and (3) the *instruction* or the work of the teacher in helping the pupils to master the subject-matter of the curriculum and adjust themselves to the organization of the school.

These factors will of necessity differ, however, according to the particular type of school in question. It will therefore be necessary to inquire [Pg 5] into the special problem of the rural school before entering into a discussion of the means by which it is to accomplish its aim.

The special problem of the rural school

Each type of school has not only its general problem which is common to all schools, but also its special problem which makes it different from every other class of schools. The special problem of any type of school grows out of the nature and needs of the community which supports the school. Thus the city school, whose pupils are to live the industrial and social life of an urban community, confronts a different problem from that of a rural school, whose pupils are to live in a farming community. Each type of school must suit its curriculum, its organization, and its instruction to the demands to be met by its pupils. The knowledge taught, the attitudes and tastes developed, and the skill acquired must be related to the life to be lived and the responsibilities to be undertaken.

The rural school must therefore be different in many respects from the town and city school. In its organization, its curriculum, and its spirit, it must be adapted to the requirements of the rural community. For, while many pupils from [Pg 6] the rural schools ultimately follow other occupations than farming, yet the primary function of the rural school is to educate for the life of the farm. It thus becomes evident that the only way to understand the problem of the rural school is first to understand the rural community. What are its industries, the character of its people, their economic status, their standards of living, their needs, their social life?

The rural community is industrially homogeneous. There exists here no such a diversified mixture of industries as in the city. All are engaged in the same line of work. Agriculture is the sole occupation. Hence the economic interests and problems all center around this one line. The success or failure of crops, the introduction of a different method of cultivation or a new variety of grain, or the invention of an agricultural implement interests all alike. The farmer engaged in planting his corn knows that for miles around all other farmers are similarly employed; if he is cutting his hay or harvesting his grain, hundreds of other mowing machines and harvesters are at work on surrounding farms.

This fund of common interest and experience tends to social as well as industrial homogeneity. Good-fellowship, social responsiveness and neigh [Pg 7] borliness rest on a basis of common labor, common problems, and common welfare. Like-mindedness and the spirit of coöperation are after all more a matter of similar occupational interests than of nationality.

Another factor tending to make the rural community socially more homogeneous than the city community is its relatively stable population, and the fact that the stream of immigration is slow in reaching the farm. It is true that the European nations are well represented among our agricultural population; but for the most part they are not foreigners of the first generation. They have assimilated the American spirit, and become familiar with American institutions. The great flood of raw immigrants fresh from widely diverse nations stops in the large centers of population, and does not reach the farm.

The prevailing spirit of democracy is still another influence favoring homogeneity in the rural community. Much less of social stratification exists in the country than in the city. Social planes are not so clearly defined nor so rigidly maintained. Financial prosperity is more likely to take the direction of larger barns and more acres than of social ostentation and exclusiveness.

America has no servile and ignorant peasan [Pg 8] try. The agricultural class constituting our rural population represents a high grade of natural intelligence and integrity. Great political and moral reforms find more favorable soil in the rural regions than in the cities. The demagogue and the "boss" find farmers impossible to control to their selfish ends. Vagabonds and idlers are out of place among them. They are a hard-headed, capable, and industrious class. As a rule, American farmers are well-to-do, not only earning a good living for their families, but constantly extending their holdings. Their farms are increasingly well improved, stocked, and supplied with labor-saving and efficient machinery. Their land is constantly growing in value, and at the same time yielding larger returns for the money and labor invested in it.

The standard of living is distinctly lower in farm homes than in town and city homes of the same financial status. The house is generally comfortable, but small. It is behind the times in many easily accessible modern conveniences possessed by the great majority of city dwellers. The bath, modern plumbing and heating, the refrigerator, and other kindred appliances can be had in the country home as well as the city. Their lack is a matter of standards rather than [Pg 9] of necessity. They will be introduced into thousands of rural homes as soon as their need is realized.

The possibilities for making the rural home beautiful and attractive are unequaled in the city for any except the very rich. It is not necessary that the farmhouse shall be crowded for space; its outlook and surroundings can be arranged to give it an æsthetic quality wholly impossible in the ordinary city home. That this is true is proved by many inexpensive farmhouses that are a delight to the eye. On the other hand, it must be admitted that a large proportion of farmhouses are lacking in both architectural attractiveness and environmental effect. Not infrequently the barns and sheds are so placed as to crowd the house into the background, and the yards for stock allowed to infringe upon the domain of the garden and the lawn. All this can be easily remedied and will be when the æsthetic taste of the dwellers on the farm comes to be offended by the incongruous and ugly.

No stinting in the abundance of food is known on the farm. The farmer supplies the tables of the world, and can himself live off the fat of the land. Grains, vegetables, meats, eggs, butter, milk, and fruits are his stock in trade. If there [Pg 10] is any lack in the farmer's table, it is due to carelessness in providing or preparing the food, and not to forced economy.

While the farming population in general live well, yet many tables are lacking in variety, especially in fruit and vegetables. Time and interest are so taken up with the larger affairs of crops and stock, that the garden goes by default in many instances. There is no market readily at hand offering fruit and vegetables for sale as in the city, and hence the farm table loses in attractiveness to the appetite and in hygienic excellence. It is probable that the prosperous city workman sits down to a better table than does the farmer, in spite of the great advantage possessed by the latter.

The population of rural communities is necessarily scattering. The nature of farming renders it impossible for people to herd together as is the case in many other industries. This has its good side, but also its bad. There are no rural slums for the breeding of poverty and crime; but on the other hand, there is an isolation and monotony that tend to become deadening in their effects on the individual. Stress and over-strain does not all come from excitement and the rush of competition; it may equally well originate in [Pg 11] lack of variety and unrelieved routine. How true this is is seen in the fact that insanity, caused in this instance chiefly by the stress of monotony, prevails among the farming people of frontier communities out of all proportion to the normal ratio.

Farming is naturally the most healthful of the industrial occupations. The work is for the greater part done in the open air and sunshine, and possesses sufficient variety to be interesting. The rural population constitutes the high vitality class of the nation, and must be constantly drawn upon to supply the brain, brawn, and nerve for the work of the city. The farmer is, on the whole, prosperous; he is therefore hopeful and cheerful, and labors in good spirit. That so many farmers and farmers' wives break down or age prematurely is due, not to the inherent nature of their work, but to a lack of balance in the life of the farm. It is not so much the work that kills, as the *continuity of the work* unrelieved by periods of rest and recreation. With the opportunities highly favorable for the best type of healthful living, no inconsiderable proportion of our agricultural population are shortening their lives and lowering their efficiency by unnecessary over-strain and failure to conform to the most funda [Pg 12] mental and elementary laws of hygienic living, especially with reference to the relief from labor that comes through change and recreation.

The rural community affords few opportunities for social recreations and amusements. Not only are the people widely separated from each other by distance, but the work of the farm is exacting, and often requires all the hours of the day not demanded for sleep. While the city offers many opportunities for choice of recreation or amusement, the country affords almost none. The city worker has his evenings, usually Saturday afternoon, and all day Sunday free to use as he chooses. Such is not the case on the farm; for after the day in the field the chores must be done, and the stock cared for. And even on Sunday, the routine must be carried out. The work of the farm has a tendency, therefore, to become much of a grind, and certainly will become so unless some limit is set to the exactions of farm labor on the time and strength of the worker. It separates the individual from his fellows in the greater part of the farm work and gives him little opportunity for social recreations or play.

One of the best evidences that the conditions of life and work on the farm need to be improved is the number of people who are leaving the [Pg 13] farm for the city. This movement has been especially rapid during the last thirty years of our history, and has continued until approximately one half our people now live in towns or cities. Not only is this loss of agricultural population serious to farming itself, creating a shortage of labor for the work of the farm, but it results in crowding other occupations already too full. There is no doubt that we have too many lawyers, doctors, merchants, clerks, and the like for the number of workers engaged in fundamental productive vocations. Smaller farms, cultivated intensively, would be a great economic advantage to the country, and would take care of a far larger proportion of our people than are now engaged in agriculture.

All students of social affairs agree that the movement of our people to towns and cities should be checked and the tide turned the other way. So important is the matter considered that a concerted national movement has recently been undertaken to study the conditions of rural life with a view to making it more attractive and so stopping the drain to the city.

Middle-aged farmers move to the town or city for two principal reasons: to educate their children and to escape from the monotony of rural [Pg 14] life. Young people desert the farm for the city for a variety of reasons, prominent among which are a desire for better education, escape from the monotony and grind of the farm life, and the opportunity for the social advantages and recreations of the city. That the retired farmer is usually disappointed and unhappy in his town home, and that the youth often finds the glamour of the city soon to fade, is true. But this does not solve the problem. The flux to the town or city still goes on, and will continue to do so until the natural desire for social and intellectual opportunities and for recreation and amusement is adequately met in rural life.

Farming as an industry has already felt the effects of a new interest in rural life. Probably no other industrial occupation has undergone such rapid changes within the last generation as has agriculture. The rapid advance in the value of land, the introduction of new forms of farm machinery, and above all the application of science to the raising of crops and stock, have almost reconstructed the work of the farm within a decade.

Special "corn trains" and "dairy trains" have traversed nearly every county in many States, teaching the farmers scientific methods. Lectur [Pg 15] ers on scientific agriculture have found their way into many communities. The Federal Government has encouraged in every way the spread of information and the development of enthusiasm in agriculture. The agricultural schools have given courses of instruction during the winter to farmers. Farmers' institutes have been organized; corn-judging and stock-judging contests have been held; prizes have been offered for the best results in the raising of grains, vegetables, or stock. New varieties of grains have been introduced, improved methods of cultivation discovered, and means of enriching and conserving the soil devised. Stock-breeding and the care of animals is rapidly becoming a science. Farming bids fair soon to become one of the skilled occupations.

Such, then, is a brief view of the situation of which the rural school is a part. It ministers to the education of almost half of the American people. This industrial group are engaged in the most fundamental of all occupations, the one upon which all national welfare and progress depend. They control a large part of the wealth of the country, the capital invested in agriculture being more than double that invested in manufactures. Agricultural wealth is rapidly increas [Pg 16] ing, both through the rise in the value of land and through improved methods of farming. The conditions of life on the farm have greatly improved during the last decade. Rural telephones reach almost every home; free mail delivery is being rapidly extended in almost every section of the country; the automobile is coming to be a part of the equipment of many farms; and the trolley is rapidly pushing out along the country roads.

Yet, in spite of these hopeful tendencies, the rural community shows signs of deterioration in many places. Rural population is steadily decreasing in proportion to the total aggregate of population. Interest in education is at a low ebb, the farm children having educational opportunities below those of any other class of our people. For, while town and city schools have been improving until they show a high type of efficiency, the rural school has barely held its own, or has, in many places, even gone backward. The rural community confronts a puzzling problem which is still far from solution.

Certain points of attack upon this problem are, however, perfectly clear and obvious. *First*, educational facilities must be improved for rural children, and their education be better adapted to farm life; *second*, greater opportunities must be [Pg 17] provided for recreation and social intercourse for both young and old; *third*, the program of farm work must be arranged to allow reasonable time for rest and recreation; *fourth*, books, pictures, lectures, concerts, and entertainments must be as accessible to the farm as to the town. These conditions must be met, not because of the dictum of any person, but because they are a fundamental demand of human nature, and must be reckoned with.

What, then, is the relation of the rural school to these problems of the rural community? How can it be a factor in their solution? What are its opportunities and responsibilities?

The adjustment of the rural school to its problem

As has been already stated, the problem of any type of school is to serve its constituency. This is to be done through relating the curriculum, the organization, and the teaching of the school to the immediate interests and needs of the people dependent on the school for their education. That the rural school has not yet fully adjusted itself to its problem need hardly be argued.

It has as good material to work upon in the boys and girls from the farm as any type of schools [Pg 18] in the country. They come of good stock; they are healthy and vigorous; and they are early trained to serious work and responsibility. Yet a very large proportion of these children possess hardly the rudiments of an education when they quit the rural school. Many of them go to school for only a few months in the year, compulsory education laws either being laxly enforced or else altogether lacking. A very small percentage of the children of the farm ever complete eight grades of schooling, and not a large proportion finish more than half of this amount.

This leaves the child who has to depend on the rural school greatly handicapped in education. He has but a doubtful proficiency in the mechanics of reading, and has read but little. He knows the elements of spelling, writing, and number, but has small skill in any of them. He knows little of history or literature, less of music, nothing of art, and has but a superficial smattering of science. Of matters relating to his life and activities on the farm he has heard almost nothing. The rural child is not illiterate, but he is too close to the border of illiteracy for the demands of a twentieth-century civilization; it is fair neither to the child nor to society.

The rural school seems in some way relatively [Pg 19] to have lost ground in our educational system. The grades of the town school have felt the stimulus of the high school for which they are preparing, and have had the care and supervision of competent administrators. The rural school is isolated and detached, and has had no adequate administrative system to care for its interests. No wonder, then, that certain grave faults in adjustment have grown up. A few of the most obvious of these faults may next claim our attention.

The rural school is inadequate in its scope. The children of the farm have as much need for education and as much right to it as those who live in towns and cities. Yet the rural school as a rule never attempts to offer more than the eight grades of the elementary curriculum, and seldom reaches this amount. It not infrequently happens that no pupils are in attendance beyond the fifth or the sixth grade. This may be due either to the small number of children in the district, or, more often, to lack of interest to continue in school beyond the simplest elements of reading, writing, and number. It is true that certain States, such as Illinois and Wisconsin, have established a system of township high schools, where secondary education equal to that to be [Pg 20] had in the cities is available to rural children. In other States a county high school is maintained for the benefit of rural school graduates. In still others, arrangements are made by which those who complete the eight grades of rural schools are received into the town high schools with the tuition paid by the rural school districts. The movement toward secondary education supplied by the rural community for its children is yet in its infancy, however, and has hardly touched the larger problem of affording adequate opportunities for the education of farm children.

The grading and organization of the rural school is haphazard and faulty. This is partly because of the small enrollment and irregular attendance, and partly because of the inexperience and lack of supervision of the teacher. Children are often found pursuing studies in three or four different grades at the same time. And even more often they omit altogether certain fundamental studies because they or their parents have a notion that these studies are unnecessary. Sometimes, owing to the small number in attendance, or to the poor classification, several grades are entirely lacking, or else they are maintained for only one or two pupils. On [Pg 21] the other hand, classes are often found following each other at an interval of only a few weeks, thereby multiplying classes until the teacher is frequently attempting the impossible task of teaching twenty-five or thirty classes a day. Children differing in age by five or six years, and possessing corresponding degrees of ability, are often found reciting in the same classes. That efficient work is impossible under these conditions is too obvious to require discussion.

The rural schools possess inadequate buildings and equipment. The average rural schoolhouse consists of one room, with perhaps a small hallway. The building is constructed without reference to architectural effect, resembling nothing so much as a large box with a roof on it. It is barren and uninviting as to its interior. The walls are often of lumber painted some dull color, and dingy through years of use. The windows are frequently dirty, and covered only by worn and tattered shades. There is usually no attempt to decorate the room with pictures, or to relieve its ugliness and monotony in any way. The library consists of a few dozens of volumes, not always supplied with a case for their protection. Of apparatus there is almost none. The work of the farm is done with efficient modern [Pg 22] equipment, the work of the farmer's school with inadequate and antiquated equipment.

While the length of the school year is increasing in the rural districts, *the term is yet much shorter than in town and city schools.* Many communities have not more than six months of school, and few more than eight. This shortage is rendered all the more serious by the irregular attendance of the rural school children. A considerable amount of absence on the part of the younger ones is unavoidable under present conditions when the distance is great and the weather bad. After all allowance is made for this fact, however, there is still an immense amount of unnecessary waste of time through non-attendance. Many rural schools show an average attendance for the year of not more than sixty per cent of the enrollment. Going to school is not yet considered a serious business by many of the rural patrons, and truant officers are not so easily available in the country as in the city.

In financial support the rural school has of necessity been behind the city school. Wealth is not piled up on a small area in agricultural communities as is the case in the city. It would often require square miles of land to equal in value certain city blocks. But making full allowance [Pg 23] for this difference, the farmers have not supported their schools as well as is done by the patrons of town and city schools. The school taxes for rural districts are much lower than in city districts, in most instances not more than half as high. It is this conservatism in expenditure that is responsible for many of the defects in the rural school, and particularly for the relatively inefficient teaching that is done. The rural teachers are the least educated, the least experienced, and the most poorly paid of any class of our teachers. They consist almost wholly of girls, a large proportion of whom are under twenty years of age, and who continue teaching not more than a year or two. Not only is this the case, but effective supervision of the teaching is wholly impossible because of the large area assigned to the county or district superintendent of rural schools. In no great industrial project should we think of placing our youngest and most inexperienced workers in the hardest and most important positions, and this without supervision of their work.

The rural school has not, therefore, yet been adjusted to its problem. It has a splendid field of work, but is not developing it. Our farming population have capacity for education and need [Pg 24] it, but they are not securing it. There is plenty of money available for the support of the rural school, but the school is not getting it. Enough well-equipped teachers can be had for the rural schools, but the standards have not yet required adequate preparation, nor the pay been sufficient to warrant extensive expenditure for it.

In the rural school is found the most important and puzzling educational problem of the present day. If our agricultural population are not to fall behind other favored classes of industrial workers in intelligence and preparation for the activities that are to engage them, the rural school must begin working out a better adjustment to its problem. Its curriculum must be broader and richer, and more closely related to the life and interests of the farm. The organization of the school, both on the intellectual and the social side, must bring it more closely into touch with the interests and needs of the rural community. The support and administration of rural education must be improved. Teachers for the rural schools must be better educated and better paid, and their teaching must be correspondingly more efficient. The following pages will be given to a discussion of these problems of adjustment.

II

THE SOCIAL ORGANIZATION OF THE RURAL SCHOOL

Every school possesses two types of organization: (1) an *intellectual* organization involving the selection and arrangement of a curriculum, and its presentation through instruction; and (2) a *social* organization involving, on the one hand, the inter-relations of the school and the community, and on the other the relations of the pupils with each other and the teacher.

The rural school and the community

The rural school and community are not at present in vital touch with each other. The community is not getting enough from the school toward making life larger, happier, and more efficient; it is not giving enough to the school either in helpful coöperation or financial support.

In general, it must be said that most of our rural people, the patrons of the rural school, have not yet conceived education broadly. They think [Pg 26] of the school as having fulfilled its function when it has supplied the simplest rudiments of reading, writing, and number. And, naturally enough, the rural school has conceived its function in the same narrow light; for it is controlled very completely by its patrons, and a stream cannot rise higher than its source.

Because of its isolation, the pressing insistence of its toil, and the monotony of its environment, the rural community is in constant danger of intellectual and social stagnation. It has far more need that its school shall be a stimulating, organizing, socializing force than has the town or city. For the city has a dozen social centres entirely outside the school: its public parks, theatres, clubs, churches, and streets, even, serve to stimulate, entertain, and educate. But the rural community is wanting in all these social forces; it is lacking in both intellectual and social stimulus and variety.

One of the most pressing needs of country districts is a common neighborhood center for both young and old, which shall stand as an organizing, welding, vitalizing force, uniting the community on a basis of common interests and activities. For while, as we have seen, the rural population as a whole are markedly homogeneous, [Pg 27] there is after all but little of common acquaintanceship and mingling among them. Thousands of rural families live lives of almost complete social isolation and lack of contact with neighbors.

This condition is one of the gravest drawbacks to farm life. The social impulse and the natural desire for recreation and amusement are as strong in country boys and girls as in their city cousins, yet the country offers young people few opportunities for satisfying these impulses and desires. The normal social tendencies of youth are altogether too strong to be crushed out by repression; they are too valuable to be neglected; and they are too dangerous to be left to take their own course wholly unguided. The rural community can never hope to hold its boys and girls permanently to the life of the farm until it has recognized the necessity for providing for the expression and development of the spontaneous social impulses of youth.

Furthermore, the social monotony and lack of variety of the rural community is a grave moral danger to its young people. It is a common impression that the great city is strewn thick with snares and pitfalls threatening to morals, but that the country is free from such temptations. The public dance halls and cheap theaters of the city [Pg 28] are beyond doubt a great and constant menace to youthful ideals and purity. But the country, going to the opposite extreme, with its almost utter lack of recreation and amusement places, offers temptations no less insidious and fatal.

The great difficulty at this point is that young people in rural communities are thrown together almost wholly in isolated pairs instead of in social groups; and that there are no objective resources of amusement or entertainment to claim their interest and attention away from themselves. They are freed from all chaperonage and the restraints of the conventions obtaining in social groups at the very time in their lives when these are most needed as steadying and controlling forces. The result is that the country districts, which ought to be of all places in the world the freest from temptation and peril to the morals of our young people, are really more dangerous than the cities. The sequel is found in the fact that a larger proportion of country girls than of city girls go astray. Nor is the rural community more successful in the morals of its boys than its girls. In other words, the lack of opportunities for free and normal social experience, the consequent ignorance of social conventions, and the absence of healthful amusement and recreation, make the [Pg 29] rural community a most unsafe place in which to rear a family.

But the necessity for social recreation and amusement does not apply to the young people alone. Their fathers and mothers are suffering from the same limitations, though of course with entirely different results. The danger here is that of premature aging and stagnation. While the toil of the city worker is relieved by change and variety, his mind rested and his mood enlivened by the stimulus from many lines of diversion, the lives of the dwellers on the farm are constantly threatened by a deadly sameness and monotony.

The indisputable tendency of farmers and their wives to age so rapidly, and so early to fall into the ranks of "fogyism," is due far more to lack of variety and recreation and to dearth of intellectual stimulus than to hard labor, severe as this often is. Age is more than the flight of the years, the stoop of the form, or the hardening of the arteries; it is also the atrophy of the intellect and the fading away of the emotions resulting from disuse. The farmer needs occasionally to have something more exciting than the alternation of the day's work with the nightly "chores." And his wife should now and then [Pg 30] have an opportunity to meet people other than those for whom she cooks and sews.

But what has all this to do with the social organization of the rural school? Much. The country cannot have its theaters, parks, and crowded thoroughfares like the city. But it needs and must have *some* social center, where its people may assemble for recreation, entertainment, and intellectual growth and development. And what is more natural and feasible than that the public school should be this center? Here is an institution already belonging to the whole people, and set apart for the intellectual training of the young. Why should it not also be made to minister to the intellectual needs of their elders as well, and to the social needs of all? *Why should not the public school building, now in use but six hours a day for little more than half the year, be open at all times when it can be helpful to any portion of the community?*

If young people are to develop naturally, if they are to make full use of their social as well as their intellectual powers, if they are to be satisfied with their surroundings, they must be provided with suitable opportunities for social mingling and recreation in groups. This is nature's way; there is no other way. The school [Pg 31] might and should afford this opportunity. There is not the least reason why the school building, when it is adapted to this purpose, should not be the common neighborhood meeting place for all sorts of young people's parties, picnics, entertainments, athletic contests, and every other form of amusement approved in the community.

Such a use of the school property would yield large returns to the community for the small additional expense required. It would serve to weld the school and community more closely together. It would vastly change the attitude of the young toward the school. It would save much of the dissatisfaction of young people with the life of the farm. It would prove a great safeguard to youthful morals. It would lead the community itself to a new sense of its duty toward the social life of the young, and to a new concept of the school as a part of the community organization. Finally, this broadened service of the school to its community would have a reflex influence on the school itself, vitalizing every department of its activities, and giving it a new vision of its opportunities.

The first obstacle that will appear in the way of such a plan is the inadequacy of the present type of country schoolhouse. And this is a seri [Pg 32] ous matter; for the barren, squalid little building of the present day would never fit into such a project. But this type of schoolhouse must go—is going. It is a hundred years behind our civilization, and wholly inadequate to present needs. Passing for later discussion the method by which these buildings are to be supplanted by better ones, let us consider further the details of the plan of making the school the neighborhood center.

First of all, each school must supply a larger area and a greater number of people than at present. It is financially impossible to erect good buildings to the number of our present schools. Nor are there pupils enough in the small district as now organized to make a school, nor people enough successfully to use the school as a neighborhood center.

Let each township, or perhaps somewhat smaller area, select a central, well-adapted site and thereon erect a modern, well-equipped school building. But this building must not be just the traditional schoolhouse with its classrooms and rows of desks. For it is to be more than a place where the children will study and recite lessons from books; it is to be the place where all the people of the neighborhood, *old and young*, will [Pg 33] assemble for entertainment, amusement, and instruction. Here will be held community picnics, social entertainments, young people's parties, lectures, concerts, debating contests, agricultural courses for the farmers, school programs, spreads and banquets, and whatever else may belong to the common social and intellectual life of the community.

The modern rural school building will therefore be home-like as well as school-like. In addition to its classrooms it will contain an assembly room capable of seating several hundred people. The seating of this room may be removable so that the floor can be cleared for social purposes or the room used for a dining-room. One or two smaller rooms will be needed for social functions, club and committee meetings. These rooms should be made attractive with good furniture, rugs, couches, and pictures. The building will contain well-equipped laboratories for manual training and domestic science, the latter of which will be found serviceable in connection with serving picnics, "spreads," and the like. The entire building should be architecturally attractive, well heated and ventilated, commodious, well furnished, and decorated with good pictures. In it should be housed a library con [Pg 34] taining several thousand well-selected books, besides magazines and newspapers. The laboratories and equipment should be fully equal to those found in the town schools, but should be adapted to the work of the rural school.

The grounds surrounding the rural school building can easily be ample in area, and beautiful in outlook and decoration. Here will be the neighborhood athletic grounds for both boys and girls, shade trees for picnics, flowers and shrubs, and ground enough for a school garden connected with the instruction in agriculture. Nor is it too much to believe that the district will in the future erect on the school grounds a cottage for the principal of the school and his family, and thus offer an additional inducement for strong, able men to devote their energies to education in the rural communities.

Now contrast this schoolhouse and equipment with the typical rural building of the present. Adjoining a prosperous farm, with its large house, its accompanying barns, silos, machine houses, and all the equipment necessary to modern farming, is the little schoolhouse. It is a dilapidated shell of a rectangular box, barren of every vestige of beauty or attractiveness both inside and out. At the rear are two outbuildings [Pg 35] which are an offense to decency and a menace to morals. Within the schoolhouse the painted walls are dingy with smoke and grime. The windows are broken and dirty, no pictures adorn the walls. The floor is washed but once or twice a year. The room is heated by an ugly box of a stove, and ventilated only by means of windows which frequently are nailed shut. The grounds present a wilderness of weeds, rubbish, and piles of ashes. It is all an outrage against the rights of the country child, and an indictment of the intelligence and ideals of a large proportion of our people.

If it is said that the plan proposed to remedy this situation is revolutionary, it will be admitted. What our rural schools of to-day need is *not improvement but reorganization*. For only in this radical way can they be made a factor in the vitalizing and conserving of the rural community which, unless some new leaven is introduced, is surely destined to disorganization and decay.

The consolidation of rural schools

The first step in reorganizing the rural schools is *consolidation*. Our rural school organization, buildings, and equipment are a full century behind our industrial and social advancement. The [Pg 36] present plan of attempting to run a school on approximately every four square miles of territory originated at a time of poverty, and when the manufacturing industries were all carried on in the homes and small shops. Our rural people are now well-to-do, and manufacturing has moved over into a well-organized set of factories; but the isolated little school, shamefully housed, meagerly equipped, poorly attended, and unskillfully taught, still remains.

Such a system of schools leaves our rural people educationally on a par with the days of cradling the grain and threshing it with a flail; of planting corn by hand and cultivating it with a hoe; of lighting the house with a tallow dip, and traveling by stage-coach.

The well-meant attempts to "improve" the rural school as now organized are futile. The proposal to solve the problem by raising the standards for teachers, desirable as this is; by the raising of salaries; or by bettering the type of the little schoolhouse, are at best but temporary makeshifts, and do not touch the root of the problem. The first and most fundamental step is to eliminate the little shacks of houses that dot our prairies every two miles along the country roads. [Pg 37]

For not only is it impossible to supply adequate buildings so near together, but it is even more impossible to find children enough to constitute a real school in such small districts. There is no way of securing a full head of interest and enthusiasm with from five to ten or twelve pupils in a school. The classes are too small and the number of children too limited to permit the organization of proper games and plays, or a reasonable variety of association through mingling together.

Furthermore, it will never be possible to pay adequate salaries to the teachers in these small schools. Nor will any ambitious and well-prepared teacher be willing to remain in such a position, where he is obliged to invest his time and influence with so few pupils, and where all conditions are so adverse.

The chief barrier to the centralization of rural education has been local prejudice and pride. In many cases a true sentimental value has attached to "the little red schoolhouse." Its praises have been sung, and orator and writer have expanded upon the glories of our common schools, until it is no wonder that their pitiful inadequacy has been overlooked by many of their patrons.

In other cases opposition has arisen to giving [Pg 38] up the small local school because of the selfish fear that the loss of the school would lower the value of adjacent property. Still others have feared that consolidation would mean higher school taxes, and have opposed it upon this ground.

But whatever the causes of the opposition to consolidation, this opposition must cease before the rural school can fulfill its function and before the rural child can have educational opportunities even approximating those given the town child. And until this is accomplished, the exodus from the farm will continue and ought to continue. Pride, prejudice, and penury must not be allowed to deprive the farm boys and girls of their right to education and normal development.

The movement toward consolidation of rural schools and transportation of the children to a central school has already attained considerable headway in many regions of the country. [1] It is now a part of the rural school system in thirty-two States. Massachusetts, the leader in consolidation, began in 1869. The movement at first grew slowly in all the States, not only having local opposition to overcome, but also meeting the problem of bad country roads interfering with the transportation of pupils.

[Pg 39] During the past half-dozen years, however, consolidation has been gaining headway, and is now going on at least five times as fast as the average for the twenty-five years preceding 1906. Indiana is at present the banner State in the rapidity of consolidation, the expenditure for conveyance having considerably more than trebled since 1904. The broad and general sweep of the movement, together with the fact that it is practically unheard of for schools that have once tried consolidation to go back to the old system, seems to indicate that the rural education of the not distant future will, except in a few regions, be carried on in consolidated schools.

The relative cost of maintaining district and consolidated schools is an important factor. Yet this factor must not be given undue prominence. It is true that the cost of education must be kept at a reasonable ratio with the standard of living of a community. But it is also true that the consolidated rural school must be looked upon as an indispensable country-life institution, and hence as having claim to a more generous basis of support than that accorded the district school.

While it is impossible, owing to such widely [Pg 40] varying conditions, to make an absolutely exact statement of the relative expense of the two types of schools, yet it has been shown in many different instances that the cost of schooling per day in consolidated schools is but slightly, if any, above that in most district schools.

The aggregate annual cost is usually somewhat higher in the consolidated schools, owing to the fact of a greatly increased attendance. A comparison made between the cost per day's schooling in the smaller district schools and consolidated schools almost invariably shows a lower expenditure for the latter. For example, the fifteen districts in Hardin County, Iowa, having in 1908 an enrollment of nine or less, averaged a cost of 27.5 cents a day for each pupil. [2] At the same time the cost per day in the consolidated rural schools of northeastern Ohio was only 17.4 cents a day, the district schools being more than fifty-seven per cent higher than the consolidated. Similar comparisons show the same trend in many other localities. In a great many of the small district schools the cost per pupil is as high as in consolidated schools where a high school course is also provided. It has been found that the average cost per year of schooling a child in a con [Pg 41] solidated school is but little above thirty dollars, while in practically all smaller district schools it far exceeds this amount, not infrequently going above fifty dollars. This means that average rural districts that are putting at least thirty dollars a year into the schooling of each child can, by consolidating their schools, secure greatly improved educational facilities with no heavier financial burden.

Not the least important of the advantages growing out of rural school consolidation is the improved attendance. Experience has shown that fully twenty-five per cent more children of school age are enrolled under the consolidated than under the district system. The advantage of this one factor alone can hardly be over-estimated, but the increase in regularity of attendance is also as great. The average daily attendance of rural schools throughout the country is approximately sixty per cent of the enrollment, and in entire States falls below fifty per cent. It has been found that consolidation, with its attendant conveyance of pupils, commonly increases the average daily attendance by as much as twenty-five per cent.

It is true that in many regions it may at present prove impossible to consolidate all the rural [Pg 42] schools. In places where the population is so sparse as to require transportation for very long distances, or where the country roads are still in such a condition in wet seasons as to be practically impassable, consolidation must of necessity be delayed. In such communities, however, the rural school need not be completely at a standstill. Much can be done to make even the one-room schoolhouse attractive and hygienic. With almost no expense, the grounds can be set with shade trees, shrubs, and perennial flowering plants. The yard can be made into a lawn in front, and into an athletic ground at the sides or the rear. Enough ground can be added to provide for all these things, and a school garden besides. The building can be rendered more inviting through better architecture, and more attention to decoration and cleanliness. An adequate supply of books and other equipment can be provided. While the isolated rural school can never take the place of the consolidated school, while it should always be looked upon as only temporarily occupying a place later to be filled by a more efficient type of school, it can after all be rendered much more efficient than it is at present. And since the one-room school will without doubt for years to come be required as a [Pg 43] supplement of the consolidated school, it should receive the same careful thought and effort toward its improvement that is being accorded the school of better type.

Financial support of the rural school

The rural school has never had adequate financial support. There has been good reason for this in many regions of the country where farm property was low in value, the land sparsely settled and not all improved, or else covered by heavy mortgages. As these conditions have gradually disappeared and the agricultural population become more prosperous, the school has in some degree shared the general prosperity. But not fully. A smaller proportion of the margin of wealth above living necessities is going into rural education now than in the earlier days of less prosperity. While the farmer has vastly "improved" his farm, he has improved his school but little. While he has been adding modern machinery and adopting scientific methods in caring for his grain and stock, his children have not had the advantage of an increasingly efficient school.

The poverty of the rural school finds its explanation in two facts: (1) the relatively low value [Pg 44] of the taxable property of the rural as compared with the town or city district, and (2) the lower rate of local school tax paid in country than in urban districts. The first of these disadvantages of the rural district cannot be remedied; but for the second, there seems to be no valid economic reason.

The approximate difference in the local school-tax rate paid in urban and rural districts is shown in the following instances, which might be duplicated from other States: —

In Kansas, the local school tax paid in 1910 by towns and cities was above eighty per cent more than that paid by country districts. In Missouri, the current report of the State Superintendent shows towns and cities seventy-five per cent higher than the country. In Minnesota, towns and cities average nearly three times the rate paid by rural districts. In Ohio, towns and cities are more than ten per cent higher than rural districts, even where the rural district maintains a full elementary and high school course. In Nebraska and Iowa, the town and city rate is about double that of country districts.

When there is added to this difference the further fact that town and city property is commonly assessed at more nearly its full value than [Pg 45] rural property, the discrepancy becomes all the greater.

It is not meant, of course, that farmers should pay as high a school-tax rate for the elementary rural school as that paid by town patrons who also have a high school available. But, on the other hand, if better school facilities are to be furnished the country children, rural property should bear its full share of the taxes required. The farmer should be willing to pay as much for the education of his child as the city dweller pays for a similar education for his.

During the last generation farmers have been increasing in wealth faster than any other class of industrial workers. Their land has doubled in value, barns have been built, machinery has been added, automobiles purchased, and large bank credits established. Yet very little of this increased prosperity has reached the school. Library, reference works, maps, charts, and other apparatus are usually lacking. In Iowa, as a fair example, a sum of not less than ten nor more than fifteen cents a year for each pupil of school age in the district is required by law to be expended for library books. Yet in not a few districts the law is a dead letter or the money grudgingly spent! In many rural schools the teacher [Pg 46] has to depend on the proceeds of a "social," an "exhibition," or a "box party" to secure a few dollars for books or pictures for the neighborhood school, and sometimes even buys brooms and dust pans from the fund secured in this way.

This is all wrong. The school should be put on a business basis. It should have the necessary tools with which to accomplish its work, and not be forced to waste the time and opportunity of childhood for want of a few dollars expended for equipment. Its patrons should realize that just as it pays to supply factory, shop, or farm with the best of instruments for carrying on the work, so it pays in the school. Cheap economy is always wasteful, and never more wasteful than when it cripples the efficiency of education.

State aid for rural schools has been proposed and in some instances tried, as a mode of solving their financial problem. Where this system has been given a fair trial, as for example in Minnesota, it has resulted in two great advantages: (1) it has encouraged the local community to freer expenditure of their own money for school purposes, since the contribution of the State is conditioned on the amount expended by the district. This is an important achievement, since it serves to train the community to the idea of more liberal [Pg 47] local taxation for school purposes, and it is probable that the greater part of the support of our schools will continue to come from this source. Another advantage of state aid is (2) that it serves to equalize educational opportunities, and hence to maintain a true educational democracy. Wealthier localities are caused to contribute to the educational facilities of those less favored, and a common advancement thereby secured.

While the theory of state aid to rural education is wholly defensible, and while it has worked well in practice, yet there is one safeguard that needs to be considered. It is manifestly unfair to ask the people of towns and cities to help pay for the support of the rural schools through the medium of the State treasury except on condition that the patrons of the rural schools themselves do their fair share. Mr. "A," living in a town where he pays twenty mills school tax, ought not to be asked to help improve Mr. "B's" rural school, while Mr. "B" is himself paying but ten mills of school tax. The farmer is as able as any one else to pay a fair rate of taxation for his school, and should be willing to do so before asking for aid from other taxation sources. Rural education must not be placed on the basis of a missionary enterprise. State aid [Pg 48] should be used to compensate for the difference in the economic *basis* for taxation in different localities, and not for a difference in the *rates* of taxation between localities equally able to pay the same rate.

We may conclude, then, that while neither the rural school nor the community has been fully aware of the possibilities for mutual helpfulness and coöperation, yet there are many hopeful signs that both are awakening to a sense of responsibility. Federal and state commissions have been created to study the rural problem, national and state teachers' associations are seeking a solution of the rural school question, and, better still, the patrons of the rural schools are in many places alive to the pressing need for better educational facilities for their children.

Growing out of these influences and the faithful work of many state and county superintendents, and not a few of the rural teachers themselves, a spirit of progress is gaining headway. Several thousand consolidated schools are now rendering excellent service to their patrons and at the same time acting as a stimulus to other communities to follow their example. State aid to rural education is no longer an experiment. [Pg 49] The people are in many localities voluntarily and gladly increasing their taxes in order that they may improve their schools. Teachers' salaries are being increased, better equipment provided, and buildings rendered more habitable.

The great educational problem of the immediate future will be to encourage and guide the movement which is now getting under way. For mistakes made now will handicap both community and school for years to come. The attempt to secure better schools by "improving" conditions in local districts should be definitely abandoned except in localities where conditions make consolidation impracticable for the present. The new consolidated school building should take definitely into account the fact that the school is to become the *neighborhood social center*, and the structure should be planned as much with this function in view as with its uses for school purposes. The new type of rural school is not to aim simply to give a better intellectual training, but is at the same time to relate this training to the conditions and needs of our agricultural population. And all who have to do with the rural schools in any way are to seek to make the school a true vitalizing factor in the community—a leaven, whose influence shall permeate every [Pg 50] line of interest and activity of its patrons and lead to a fuller and richer life.

The rural school and its pupils

One of the surest tests of any school is the attitude of the pupils—the spirit of loyalty, coöperation, and devotion they manifest with reference to their education. Do they, on the whole, look upon the school as an opportunity or an imposition? Do they consider it *their* school, and make its interests and welfare their concern, or do they think of it as the teacher's school, or the board's school or the district's school? These questions are of supreme importance, for the question of attitude, quite as much as that of ability, determines the use made of opportunity.

It must be admitted that throughout our entire school system there remains something to be desired in the spirit of coöperation between pupils and schools. The feeling of loyalty which the child has for his home does not extend commensurately to the school. Too often the school is looked upon as something forced upon the child, for his welfare, perhaps, but after all not as forming an interesting and vital part of his present experience. It is often rather a place where so much time and effort and inconven [Pg 51] ience must be paid for so many grades and promotions, and where, incidentally, preparation is supposed to be made for some future demands very dimly conceived. At best, there is frequently a lack of feeling of full identity of interests between the child and the school.

The youth, immaturity, and blindness of childhood make it impossible, of course, for children to conceive of their school in a spirit of full appreciation. On the other hand, the very nature of childhood is responsiveness and readiness of coöperation in any form of interesting activity,—is loyalty of attitude toward what is felt to minister to personal happiness and well-being. In so far, therefore, as there exists any lack of loyalty and coöperation of pupils toward their school, the reasons for such defection are to be sought first of all in the school, and not in the child.

While this negative attitude of the pupils exists in some degree in all our schools, it is undoubtedly more marked in our rural schools than in others. In a negligible number of cases does this lack of coöperation take the form of overt rebellion against the authority of the school. It is manifested in other ways, many of them wholly unconscious to the child, as, for example, [Pg 52] lack of desire to attend school, and indifference to its activities when present.

Attending school is the most important occupation that can engage the child. Yet the indifference of children and their parents alike to the necessity for schooling makes the small and irregular attendance of rural school pupils one of the most serious problems with which educators have to deal. County superintendents have in many places offered prizes and diplomas with the hope of bettering attendance, but such incentives do not reach the source of the difficulty. The remedy must finally lie in a fundamental change of attitude toward the school and its opportunities. Good attendance must spring from interest in the school work and a feeling of its value, rather than from any artificial incentives.

How great a problem poor attendance at rural schools is, may be realized from the fact that, in spite of compulsory education laws, not more than seventy per cent of the children accessible to the rural school are enrolled, and of this number only about sixty per cent are in daily attendance. This is to say that under one half of our farm children are daily receiving the advantages of even the rural school. In some States this proportion will fall as low as three tenths instead [Pg 53] of one half. In many rich agricultural counties of the Middle West, having a farming population of approximately ten thousand, not more than forty or fifty pupils per year complete the eight grades of the rural school.

If the rural school is to be able to claim the regular attendance and spontaneous coöperation of the children it must (1) be reasonably accessible to them, (2) be attractive and interesting in itself, and (3) offer work the value and application of which are evident.

The inaccessibility of the rural school has always been one of its greatest disadvantages. In a large proportion of cases, a walk of from a mile to a mile and a half along country roads or across cultivated fields has been required to reach the schoolhouse. During inclement weather, or when deep snow covers the ground, this distance proves almost prohibitive for all the smaller children. Wet feet and drenched clothing have been followed by severe colds, coughs, bronchitis, or worse, and the children have not only suffered educationally, but been endangered physically as well.

It has been found in all instances that public conveyance of pupils to the consolidated schools greatly increases rural school patronage. It makes [Pg 54] the school accessible. The regular wagon service does away with the "hit-and-miss" method of determining for each succeeding day whether it is advisable for the child to start for school. So important is this factor in securing attendance, that a careful study by Knorr [3] of the attendance in Ohio district and consolidated schools shows twenty-seven per cent more of the total school population in school under the influence of public conveyance and other features peculiar to consolidation than under the district system. He concludes that, broadly speaking, by a system of consolidated schools with public conveyance, rural school attendance can be increased by at least one fourth.

The life in the typical rural school is not sufficiently interesting and attractive to secure a strong hold upon the pupils. The dreary ugliness of the physical surroundings has already been referred to. And even in districts where the building and grounds have been made reasonably attractive, there is yet wanting a powerful factor — the influence of the social incentive that comes from numbers. In hundreds of our rural schools the daily attendance is less than a dozen pupils, frequently not representing more than three or four families. The classes can therefore [Pg 55] contain not more than two or three pupils, and often only one. There is no possibility of organizing games, or having the fun and frolic possible to larger groups of children. Add to this the fact that the teaching is often spiritless and uninspiring, and the reason becomes still more plain why so many rural children drop out of school with scarcely the rudiments of an education.

Here, again, the consolidated school, with its attractive building, its improved equipment, its larger body of pupils, and its better teaching, appears as a solution of the difficulty. For it does what the present type of district school can never do—it makes school life interesting and attractive to its pupils, and this brings to bear upon them one of the strongest incentives to continue in school and secure an education.

Finally, much of the work of the school has not appealed to the pupils as interesting or valuable. This has not been altogether the fault of the curriculum, but often has come from the lack of adaptability of the work to the pupils studying it. Through frequent changes of teachers, poor classification, and irregularity of attendance, rural pupils have often been forced to go over and over the same ground, without any reference [Pg 56] to whether they were ready to advance or not. In other cases, careless grading has placed children in studies for which they were utterly unprepared, and from which they could get nothing but discouragement and dislike for school. In still other instances the course pursued has been ill-balanced, and in no degree correlated. Often the whim of the child determines whether he will or will not study certain subjects, the teacher lacking either the knowledge or insistence to bring about a better organization of the work.

The unskilled character of the rural school-teaching force, and the impossibility of securing any reasonable supervision as the system is at present organized, make us again turn to the consolidated school as the remedy for these adverse conditions. For with its improved attendance, its skilled teaching, and its better supervision, it easily and naturally renders such conditions impossible. Give the consolidated school, in addition, the greatly enriched curriculum which it will find possible to offer its pupils, and the vexing question of the relation of the rural school to its pupils will be far toward solution.

Let us next consider somewhat in detail the curriculum of the rural school.

FOOTNOTES:

[1] See "Consolidated Rural Schools," Bulletin 232, U. S. Department of Agriculture.

[2] Bulletin 232, U. S. Department of Agriculture, p. 38.

[3] Bulletin 232, U. S. Department of Agriculture, p. 51.

III

THE CURRICULUM OF THE RURAL SCHOOL

If we grant the economic ability to support good schools, then the curriculum offered by any type of school, the scope of subject-matter given the pupils to master, is a measure of the educational ideals of those maintaining and using the schools. If the curriculum is broad, and representative of the various great fields of human culture; if it relates itself to the life and needs of its patrons; if it is adapted to the interests and activities of its pupils, it may be said that the people believe in education as a right of the individual and as a preparation for successful living. But if, on the other hand, the curriculum is meager and narrow, consisting only of the rudiments of knowledge, and not related to the life of the people or the interests of the pupils, then it may well be concluded that education is not highly prized, that it is not understood, or that it is looked upon as an incidental.

The scope of the rural school curriculum

Modern conditions require a broader and more [Pg 58] thorough education than that demanded by former times, and far more than the typical district rural school affords. The old-time school offered only the "three R's," and this was thought sufficient for an education. But these times have passed. Not only has society greatly increased in wealth during the last half-century, but it has also grown much in intelligence. Many more people are being educated now than formerly, and they are also being vastly better educated. For the concept of what constitutes an education has changed, and the curriculum has grown correspondingly broader and richer.

It is therefore no longer possible to express the educational status of a community in the percentage of people who can merely read and write. Educational progress has become a national ideal. The elementary schools in towns and cities have been greatly strengthened both in curriculum and teaching. High schools have been organized and splendidly equipped, and their attendance has rapidly increased.

But all this development has hardly touched the rural school. The curriculum offered is pitifully narrow even for an elementary school, and very few high schools are supported by rural communities. In fact, a large proportion of our rural [Pg 59] population are receiving an education but little in advance of that offered a hundred years ago in similar schools. This is not fair to the children born and reared on the farm; it is not fair to one of the greatest and most important industries of our country; and it cannot but result disastrously in the end.

If the rural school is to meet its problem, it must extend the scope of its curriculum. It was formerly thought by many that education, except in its simplest elements, was only for those planning to enter the "learned professions." But this idea has given way before the onward sweep of the spirit of democracy, and we now conceive education as the right and duty of *all*. Nor by education do we mean the simple ability to read, write, and number.

Our present-day civilization demands not only that the child shall be taught to read, but also that he shall be supplied with books and guided in his reading. Through reading as a tool he is to become familiar with the best in the world's literature and its history. He is not only to learn number, but is to be so educated that he may employ his number concepts in fruitful ways. He must not only be familiar with the mechanics of writing, but must have knowledge, interests, [Pg 60] experience that will give him something to write about. The "three R's" are necessary tools, but they are only tools, and must be utilized in putting the child into possession of the best and most fruitful culture of the race. And, practically, they must put him into command of such phases of culture as touch his own life and experience and make him more efficient.

The rural school cannot extend the scope of its curriculum simply by inserting in the present curriculum new studies related to the life and work of the farm. The modification must be deeper and more thoroughgoing than this. *A full elementary course of eight years and a high school course of four years should be easily accessible to every rural child.* Less than this amount of education is inadequate to prepare for the life of the farm, and fails to put the individual into full possession of his powers. Nor, in most instances, should the high schooling be left to some adjacent town, which is to receive the rural pupils upon payment of tuition to the town district. Unless the town is small, and practically a part of the rural community, it cannot supply, either in the subject-matter of the curriculum or the spirit of the school, the type of education that the rural children should have. For in so far as [Pg 61] the town or city high school leads to any specific vocation, it certainly does not lead toward industrial occupations, and least of all toward agriculture. It rather prepares for the professions, or for business careers. Its tendency is very strongly to draw the boys and girls away from the farm instead of preparing them for it.

While the rural child, therefore, must be provided with a better and broader education, he should usually not be sent to town to get it. If he is, the chances are that he will stay in town and be lost to the farm. Indeed, this is precisely what has been happening; the town or city high school has been turning the country boy away from the farm. For not only does what one studies supply his knowledge; it also determines his *attitude*.

If the curriculum contains no subject-matter related to the immediate experience and occupation of the pupil, his education is certain to entice him away from his old interests and activities. The farm boy whose studies lack all point of contact with his life and work will soon either lose interest in the curriculum or turn his back upon the farm. If the boys and girls born on the farm are to be retained in this form of industry, the rural school must be broadened to give them [Pg 62] an education equal to that afforded by town or city for its youth. If the rural community cannot accomplish this end, it has no claim on the loyalty and service of its youth. Rural children have a right to a well-organized, well-equipped, and well-taught elementary school of eight years and a high school of four years, with a curriculum adapted especially to their interests and needs.

It is not meant, of course, that the rural school, with its present organization and administration, can extend the scope of its curriculum to make it the equal of that offered in the grades of the town or city school. Radical changes, such as those discussed in the preceding chapter, will have to be made in the rural district system before this is possible. That these changes are being made and the full elementary and high school course offered in many consolidated rural schools, scattered from Florida to Idaho, is proof both of the feasibility of the plan and of an awakened public demand for better rural education.

The broadened curriculum of the rural school must contain subject-matter especially related to the interests and activities of the farm; upon this all are agreed. But it must not stop with vocational subjects alone. For, while one's vocation is fundamental, it is not all of life. Education [Pg 63] should help directly in making a living; it must also help to live. Broad and permanent lines of interest must be set up and trained to include many forms of experience. The child must come to know something of the great social institutions of his day and of the history leading to their development. He must become familiar with the marvelous scientific discoveries and inventions underlying our modern civilization. He must be led to feel appreciation for the beautiful in art, literature, and music; and must have nurtured in his life a love for goodness and truth in every form. In short, through the curriculum the latent powers constituting the life capital of every normal child are to be stimulated and developed to the end that his life shall be more than mere physical existence—to the end that it shall be crowned with fullness of knowledge, richness of feeling, and the victory of worthy achievement. This is the right of every child in these prosperous and enlightened times,—the right of the country child as well as the city child. And society will not have done its duty in providing for the education of its youth until the children of the farm have full opportunities for such development.

The rural elementary school curriculum

[Pg 64]

By the elementary school is meant the eight grades of work below the high school which the rural school is now meant to cover.

Whatever is put into the curriculum of a nation's schools finally becomes a part of national character and achievement. What the children study in school comes to determine their attitudes and shape their aptitudes. The old Greek philosophers, becoming teachers of youth, turned the nation into a set of students and disputants over philosophical questions. Sparta taught her boys the arts of war, and became the chief military nation of her time. Germany introduces technological studies into her schools, and becomes the leading country in the world in the arts of manufacture. Let any people emphasize in their schools the studies that lead to commercial and professional interests, and neglect those that prepare for industrial vocations, and the industrial welfare of the nation is sure to suffer.

The curriculum of the rural school must, therefore, contain the basic subjects that belong to all culture,—the studies that every normal, intelligent person should have just because he belongs to the twentieth-century civilization, and in addi [Pg 65] tion must include the subjects that afford the knowledge and develop the attitude and technique belonging to the life of the farm. Let us now consider this curriculum somewhat more in detail.

The mother tongue. Mastery of his mother tongue is the birthright of every child. He should first of all be able to speak it correctly and with ease. He should next be able to read it with comprehension and enjoyment, and should become familiar with the best in its literature. He should be able to write it with facility, both as to its spelling and its composition. Finally, he should know something of the structure, or grammar, of the language.

This requirement suggests the content of the curriculum as to English. The child must be given opportunity to use the language orally; he must be led to talk. But this implies that he must have something to say, and be interested in saying it. Formal "language lessons," divorced from all the child's interests and activities, will not meet the purpose. Facility in speech grows out of enthusiasm in speaking. Every recitation is a lesson in English, and should be used for this purpose; nor should the aim be correctness only, but ease and fluency as well.

The child must also learn to read; not alone [Pg 66] to pronounce the printed words of a page, but to grasp the thought and feeling, and express them in oral reading. This presupposes a mastery of the mechanics of reading, the letters, words, and marks employed. The only way to learn to read is by reading. This is true whether we refer to learning the mechanics of reading, to learning the apprehension and expression of thought, or to learning the art of appreciating and enjoying good literature.

Yet, trite and self-evident as this truism is, it is constantly violated in teaching reading in the rural school. For the course in reading usually consists of a series of five readers, expected to cover seven or eight years of study. These readers contain less than one hundred pages of reading matter to the year, or but little more than half a page a day for the time the child should be in school. The result is that the same reader is read over and over, to no purpose. With a rich literature available for each of the eight years of the elementary school, comparatively few of the rural schools have supplied either supplementary readers or other reading books for the use of the children.

The result is that most rural school children learn to read but stumblingly, and seldom attain [Pg 67] sufficient skill and taste in reading so that it becomes a pleasure. Such a situation as this indicates the same lack of wisdom that would be shown in employing willing and skillful workmen to garner a rich harvest, and then sending them into the fields with wholly insufficient and inadequate tools. The rural school must not only teach the child the mechanics of reading, but lead him to read and love good books. This can be done only *by supplying the books and giving the child an opportunity to read them.*

Comparatively few people like to write. The pathway of expression finds its way out more easily through the tongue than through the hand. Yet it is highly necessary that every one should in this day be able to write. Nor does this mean merely the ability to form letters into words and put them down with a pen so that they are legible. This is a fundamental requisite, but the mastery of penmanship, spelling, and punctuation is, however, only a beginning. One must be able to formulate his thoughts easily, to construct his sentences correctly, and to make his writing effective; he must learn the art of composition.

Here again the principle already stated applies. The way to learn to write is by writing; [Pg 68] not just by the dreary treadmill of practicing upon formal "compositions," but by having something to write that one cares to express. The written language lessons should, therefore, always grow out of the real interests and activities of the child in the home, the school, or on the farm, and should include the art of letter-writing, argumentation and exposition, as well as narration and description.

The subject of formal grammar has little or no place in the grades of the elementary school. The grammatical relations of the language are complicated and beyond the power of the child at an early age. Nor does the study of such relations result in efficiency in the use of language, as is commonly supposed. Children are compelled in many schools to waste weary years in the study of logical relations they are too young to comprehend, when they should be reading, speaking, and writing their mother tongue under the stimulus and guidance of a teacher who is himself a worthy and enthusiastic model in the use of speech. Only the simpler grammatical forms and relations should be taught in the grades, and these should have immediate application to oral and written speech.

Arithmetic. Arithmetic has for more than two [Pg 69] hundred years formed an important part of the elementary school curriculum. It has been taught with the double object of affording mental discipline for the child, and of putting him into possession of an important tool of practical knowledge. It is safe to say that a large proportion of the patrons of the rural schools of the present look upon arithmetic as the most important subject taught in the school after the simple mechanics of reading. Ability to "cipher" has been thought of as constituting a large and important part of the educational equipment of the practical man.

Without doubt, number is an essential part of the education of the child. Yet there is nothing in the mere art of numbering things as we meet them in daily experience that should make arithmetic require so large a proportion of time as it has been receiving. The child is usually started in number in the first grade, and continues it the full eight years of the elementary course, finally devoting three or more years of the high school course to its continued study. Thus, nearly one fourth of the entire school time of the pupil is demanded by the various phases of the number concept.

The only ground upon which the expenditure [Pg 70] of this large proportion of time upon number can be defended is that of *disci-*

pline. And modern psychology and experimental pedagogy have shown the folly and waste of setting up empty discipline as an educational aim. Education time is too short, and the amount of rich and valuable material waiting to be mastered too great, to devote golden years to a relatively barren grind.

It is probable that at least half the time at present devoted to arithmetic in the elementary school could be given to other subjects with no loss to the child's ability in number, and with great gain to his education as a whole. Not that the child knows number any too well now. He does not. In fact, few children finishing the elementary school possess any considerable degree of ability in arithmetic. They can work rather hard problems, if they have a textbook, and the answers by which to test their results. But give them a practical problem from the home, the farm, or the shop, and the chances are two to one that they cannot secure a correct result. This is not the fault of the child, but the fault of the kind of arithmetic he has been given, and the way it has been taught. We have taught him the solution of various difficult, analytical problems not in the least typical of the concrete [Pg 71] problems to be met daily outside of school; but we have not taught him to add, subtract, multiply, and divide with rapidity and accuracy. We have required him to solve problems containing fractions with large and irreducible denominators such as are never met in the business world, but he cannot readily and with certainty handle numbers expressed in halves, thirds, quarters, fifths, and eighths. He has been compelled to sacrifice practical business efficiency in number to an attempt to train his powers of logical analysis.

The arithmetic of the district school should be greatly simplified and reduced in quantity. Its quality should be greatly improved both as to accuracy and speed in the fundamental operations and in the various concrete types of problems to be met in the home, on the farm, and in the shop. There need be no fear that the mental training will be less efficient with this type of arithmetic. For mental development comes only where there is mastery, and there is no mastery of the arithmetic as it is taught in the rural school to-day.

History and civics. Every American child should know the history and mode of government of his country. This is true first of all because this knowledge is necessary to intelligent partici [Pg 72] pation in the affairs of a republic; but it is also necessary to the right development of the individual that he shall realize something of the heroism and sacrifice required to produce the civilization which he enjoys. Every person needs to extend his thought and appreciation until it is large enough to include other peoples and times than his own. For only in this way can he come to feel kinship with the race at large, and thus save himself from provincialism and narrowness.

This is equivalent to saying that the curriculum should afford ample opportunity for the study of history. Nor should the history given the child deal chiefly with the military and political activities of the nation. Many text books have been little more than an account of wars and politics. These are not the aspects of national life that most interest and concern the child, especially at the age when he is in the elementary school. He should at this time be told about the *people* of his country,—their home life, their industries, their schools and churches, their bravery, their hardships, adventures, and achievements. He must come to know something of the great men and women of his Nation and State, the writers, inventors, explorers, scientists, [Pg 73] artists, and musicians, as well as the soldiers and statesmen.

Not only does this require that the child shall have suitable text-books in history, but that he shall also have an adequate library of interesting histories, biographies, and historical fiction adapted to his age and interests. For it is not enough that the child shall learn the elementary facts of history while he is in the elementary school; more important still is it that he shall develop a real interest in history, and form the taste for reading historical matter.

The course in history must, therefore, contain such matter as the child will love to read; for only then will it leave the desire to read. It must so put a premium upon patriotism, loyalty to country, and high-grade citizenship that the child shall feel the impulse to emulate the noble men and women who have contributed to our happiness and welfare. The study of history, even in the elementary school, should eventuate in loyal, efficient citizenship.

The civics taught in the elementary school should be very practical and concrete. The age has not yet come for a study of the federal or state constitution. It is rather the *functional* aspect of government that should be presented at [Pg 74] this time—the points of contact of school district, township, county, state and federal government with the individual. How the school is supported and controlled; how the bridges are built and roads repaired; the work of township and county affairs; the powers and duties of boards of health; the right of franchise and the use of the ballot; the work of the postal system; the making and enforcing of laws,—these and similar topics suggest what the child should come to know from the study of civics. The great problem here is to influence conduct in the direction of upright citizenship, and to give such a knowledge of the machinery, especially of local government, as will lead to efficient participation in its activities.

Geography and nature study. The rural school has a great advantage over the city school in the teaching of geography and nature study. For the country child is closer to the earth and its products than the city child. The broad expanse of nature is always before him; life in its multiple forms constantly appeals to his eye and ear. He watches the seeds planted, and sees the crops cultivated and harvested. He has a very concrete sense of the earth as the home of man, and possesses a basis of practical knowledge for [Pg 75] understanding the resources and products of his own and other countries.

Geography should, therefore, be one of the most vital and useful branches in the rural school. It is to begin wherever the life of the child touches nature in his immediate environment, and proceed from this on out to other parts of his home land, and finally to all lands.

But the geography taught must not be of the old catechism type, which resulted in children committing to memory the definitions of geographical terms instead of studying the real objects ready at hand. It must not concern itself with the pupil's learning the names and locations of dozens of places and geographical forms of no particular importance, instead of coming into immediate touch with natural environment and with the earth in the larger sense as it bears upon his own life. The author has expressed this idea in another place as follows:—

"The content of geography is, therefore, synonymous with the content of the experience of the child as related to his own interests and activities, in so far as they grow out of the earth as his home. Towns and cities begin with the ones nearest at hand. The concept of rivers has its rise in the one that flows past the child's home. [Pg 76] Valleys, mountains, capes, and bays are but modifications of those that lie within the circle of personal experience. Generalizations must come to be made, but they must rest upon concrete and particular instances if they are to constitute a reality to the learner.

"What kind of people live in a country, what they work at, what they eat, and how they live in their homes and their schools, what weather they have, and what they wear, how they travel and speak and read,—these are more vital questions to the child than the names and locations of unimportant streams, towns, capes, and bays. For they are the things that touch his own experience, and hence appeal to his interest. Only as geography is given this social background, and concerns itself with the earth as related to social activities, can it fulfill its function in the elementary school." [4]

Hygiene and health. Since health is at the basis of all success and happiness, nothing can be more important in the education of the child than the subject of practical hygiene. It has been the custom in our schools until recently, however, to give the child a difficult and uninteresting text book dealing with physiology and anatomy, but [Pg 77] containing almost nothing on hygiene and the laws of health.

Not only should the course in physiology emphasize the laws of hygiene, but this hygiene should in part have particular bearing on right living under the conditions imposed by the farm. Food, its variety, adaptability, and preparation; clothing for the different seasons; work, recreation, and play; care of the eyes and teeth; bathing; the ventilation of the home, and especially of sleeping-rooms; the effects of tobacco and cigarettes in checking growth and reducing efficiency; the more simple and obvious facts bearing on the relation of bacteria to the growth, preparation, and spoiling of foods; the means to be taken to prevent bacterial contagion of diseases,—these are some of the practical matters that every child should know as a result of his study of physiology and hygiene.

But we must go one step further still. It is not enough to teach these things as matters of abstract theory or truth. Plenty of people know better hygiene than they are practicing. The subject must be presented so concretely and effectively and be supported by such incentives that it will actually lead to better habits of living — that it will *result in higher physical efficiency*. [Pg 78]

Agriculture. Agriculture is of course preeminently a subject for the rural school. Not only is it of immediate and direct practical importance, but it is coming to be looked upon as so useful a cultural study that it is being introduced into many city schools.

It has been objected that agriculture as a science cannot be taught in the elementary school because of the lack of age and development of the pupils. This is true, but neither can any other subject be taught to children of this age as a complete science. It is possible, however, to give children in the rural elementary school much useful information concerning agriculture. Perhaps better still, it is possible to develop a scientific attitude and interest that will lead to further study of the subject in the high school or agricultural college, and that will in the mean-time serve to attach the boys and girls to the farm.

The rural school pupils can be made familiar with the best modes of planting and cultivating the various crops, and with the diseases and insect enemies which threaten them; the selection of seed; the rotation of crops, and many other practical things applying directly to their home life. School gardens of vegetables and flowers [Pg 79] constitute another center of interest and information, and serve to unite the school and the home.

Similarly the animal life of the farm can be studied, and a knowledge gained of the best varieties of farm stock, their breeding and care. Insects and bird life can be observed, and their part in the growth or destruction of crops understood. All this is not only practicable, but necessary as part of the rural school curriculum. Anything less than this amount of practical agriculture leaves the rural school in some degree short of fulfilling its function.

Domestic science and manual training. In general what is true of agriculture is true of domestic science and manual training. They can be presented in the elementary school only in the most concrete and applied form. But they can be successfully presented in this form, and must be if the rural school child is to have an equal opportunity with the town and city child. The girls can be taught the art of sewing, cooking, and serving, if only the necessary equipment and instruction are available. They are ready to learn, the subject-matter is adapted to their age and understanding, and nothing could be more vital to their interests and welfare. [Pg 80]

Likewise the boys can be taught the use of tools, the value and finishing of different kinds of woods, and can develop no little skill with their hands, while they are at the same time receiving mental development and the cultivation of practical interests from this line of work. It is not in the least a question of the readiness of the boys to take up and profit by this subject, but is only a matter of equipment and teaching.

Music and art. Nor should the finer aspects of culture be left out of the education of the country child. He will learn music as readily as the city child, and love it not less. Indeed, he needs it even more as a part of his schooling, since the opportunities to hear and enjoy music are always at hand in the city, and nearly always lacking in the country. The child should be taught to sing and at least to understand and appreciate music of worthy type.

The same principle will apply to art. The great masterpieces of painting and sculpture have as much of beauty and inspiration in them as the great masterpieces of literature. Yet most rural children complete their schooling hardly having seen in the schoolroom a worthy copy of a great picture, and much less have they been taught the [Pg 81] significance of great works of art or been led to appreciate and love them.

Physical training. It has been argued by many that the rural child has enough exercise and hence does not need physical training. But this position entirely misconceives the purpose of physical training. One may have plenty of exercise, even too much exercise, without securing a well-balanced physical development. Indeed, certain forms of farm work done by children are often so severe a tax on their strength that a corrective exercise is necessary in order to save stooped forms, curved spines, and hollow chests. Furthermore, the farm child, lacking the opportunities of the city child for gaining social ease and control, needs the development that comes from physical training to give poise, ease of bearing, and grace of movement.

Nor must the athletic phase of physical training be overlooked. While it is undoubtedly true that athletics have come to occupy too large a part of the time and absorb too great a proportion of the interest in many schools, yet this is no reason for omitting avocational training wholly from the rural school. Children require the training and development that come from games and play quite as much as they need that coming [Pg 82] from work. The school owes a duty to the avocational side of life as well as to the vocational.

The curriculum here proposed is so much broader and richer than that now offered in the rural district school that it will appear to many to be visionary and impossible. That it is impossible for the old type of rural school will be readily admitted. But it is entirely practicable and possible in the reorganized consolidated school, and is being successfully presented, in its general aspects, at least, in many of these schools. It is only such an education as every rural child is entitled to, and is no more than the urban child is already receiving in the better class of town and city elementary schools. If the rural school cannot give the farm child an elementary education approximating the one out-lined, it has no claim on his loyalty or time; and he should in justice to himself be taken where he can receive a worthy education, even if he is thereby lost to the farm.

But the rural boy and girl need not only a good elementary education, but a high school education as well. Let us next consider the rural high school curriculum.

The rural high school curriculum

[Pg 83]

This section is presented in the full knowledge that comparatively few localities have as yet established the rural high school. It now forms, however, an integral part of the consolidated rural school in not a few places, and is abundantly justifying the expenditure made upon it. In other localities the tendency is growing to send the rural child to the town high school, or even for the family to move to town to secure high schooling for the children. In still other cases, and we are obliged to admit that these yet constitute the rule rather than the exception, the farm boy or girl has no opportunity for a high school education.

If we succeed in working out the so-called rural problem of our country, in maintaining a high standard of agricultural population and rural life, the rural high school must be an important factor in our problem. For the children of our farms need and must have an education reaching beyond that of the elementary school. And this schooling must prepare them to find the most satisfactory and successful type of life on the farm, instead of drawing them away from the farm. [Pg 84]

It goes without saying that the rural high school should be an agricultural high school. This does not mean that it shall devote itself exclusively to teaching agriculture; but rather that, while it offers a broad range of culture and information, it shall emphasize those phases of subject-matter that will best fit into the interests and activities of farm life, instead of those phases that tend to lead toward the city or the market-place. Its four years of work must be fully equal to that of the best town or city high schools, but must in some degree be different work. It must result in *efficiency*, and efficiency here must relate itself to agricultural life and pursuits.

A detailed discussion of the rural high school curriculum will not be required. The principles already suggested as applying to the elementary school will govern here as well. The studies must cultivate breadth of view and a wide range of interests, and must at the same time bear upon the immediate life and experience of the pupils. The lines of study begun in the elementary school will be continued, with the purpose of securing deeper insight, more detailed knowledge, and greater independence of judgment and action.

English should form an important part of the [Pg 85] curriculum, with the double aim of securing facility in the use of the mother tongue and of developing a love for its literature. The rural high school graduate should be able to write English correctly as to spelling, punctuation, and grammar; he should be able to express himself effectively, either in writing, conversation, or the more formal speech of the rostrum. Above all, he should be an enthusiastic and discriminating reader, with a catholicity of taste and interest that will lead him beyond the agricultural journal and newspaper, important as these are, to the works of fiction, material and social science, travel and biography, current magazines and journals, and whatever else belongs to the intellectual life of an intelligent, educated man of affairs.

This is asking more than is being accomplished at present by the course in English in the town high school, but not more than is easily within the range of possibility. The average high school graduate of to-day cannot always spell and punctuate correctly, and commonly cannot write well even an ordinary business letter; nor, it must be feared, has his study of literature had a very great influence in developing him into a good reader of worthy books. [Pg 86]

But all this can be remedied by vitalizing the teaching of the mother tongue; by lessening the proportion of time and emphasis placed upon critical analysis and technical literary criticism, and increasing that given to the drill and practice that alone can make sure of the fundamentals of spelling, punctuation, and the common forms of composition emphasized by all; and by the sympathetic, enthusiastic teaching of good literature adapted to the age and interests of the pupils from the standpoint of synthetic appreciation and enjoyment, rather than from the standpoint of mechanical analysis.

The rural high school course in social science should be broad and thorough. The course in history should not give an undue proportion of time to ancient and medieval history, nor to war and politics. Emphasis should be placed on the social, industrial, and economic phases of human development in modern times and in our own country.

Political economy should form an important branch. Especially should it deal with the problems of production, distribution, and consumption as they relate to agriculture. Matters of finance, taxation, and investment, while resting on general principles, should be applied to the [Pg 87] problems of the farm. Nor should the economic basis of support and expenditure in the home be overlooked.

The course in civics should not only present the general theory of government, but should apply concretely to the civic relations and duties of a rural population. Especially should it appeal to the civic conscience and sense of responsibility which we need among our rural people to make the country an antidote to the political corruption of the city.

Material science should constitute an important section of the rural high school curriculum. Not only does its study afford one of the best means of mental development, but the subject-matter of science has a very direct bearing on the life and industries of the farm. To achieve the best results, however, the science taught must be presented from the concrete and applied point of view rather than from the abstract and general. This does not mean that a hodge-podge of unrelated facts shall be taught in the place of science; indeed, such a method would defeat the whole purpose of the course. It means, however, that the general laws and principles of science shall be carried out to their practical bearing on the problems of the home and the farm, and not [Pg 88] be left just as general laws or abstract principles unapplied.

The botany and zoölogy of the rural high school will, of course, have a strong agricultural trend. It will sacrifice the old logical classifications and study of generic types of animals and plants for the more interesting and useful study of the fauna and flora of the locality. The various farm crops, their weed enemies, the helpful and harmful insects and birds, the animal life of the barnyard, horticulture and floriculture, and the elements of bacteriology, will constitute important elements in the course.

The course in physics will develop the general principles of the subject, and will then apply these principles to the machinery of the farm, to the heating, lighting, and ventilation of houses, to the drainage of soil, the plumbing of buildings, and a hundred other practical problems bearing on the life of the farm. Chemistry will be taught as related to the home, foods, soils, and crops. A concrete geology will lead to a better understanding of soils, building materials, and drainage. Physiology and hygiene will seek as their aim longer life and higher personal efficiency.

The course in agriculture, whether presented separately or in conjunction with botany and [Pg 89] zoölogy, must be comprehensive and thorough. Not only should it give a complete and practical knowledge of the selection of seed; the planting, cultivating, and harvesting of crops; the improvement and conservation of the soil; the breeding and care of stock, etc., but it must serve to create and develop a scientific attitude toward farming. The farmer should come to look upon his work as offering the largest opportunities for the employment of technical knowledge, judgment, and skill. That such an attitude will yield large returns in success is attested by many farmers to-day who are applying scientific methods to their work.

Manual training and domestic science should receive especial emphasis in the rural high school. Both subjects have undoubted educational value in themselves, and their practical value and importance to those looking forward to farm life can hardly be overestimated. And in these as in other subjects, the course offered will need to be modified from that of the city school in order to meet the requirements of the particular problems to which the knowledge and training secured are to be applied.

Mathematics should form a part of the rural high school curriculum, but the traditional courses [Pg 90] in algebra and geometry do not meet the need. The ideal course would probably be a skillful combination of algebra, geometry, and trigonometry occupying the time of one or two years, and applied directly to the problems of mechanics, measurements, surveying, engineering, and building on the farm. Such an idea is not new, and textbooks are now under way providing material for such a course.

In addition, there should be a thorough course in practical business arithmetic. By this is not meant the abstract, analytical matter so often taught as high school arithmetic, but concrete and applied commercial and industrial arithmetic, with particular reference to farm problems. In connection with this subject should be given a course in household accounts, and book-keeping, including commercial forms and commercial law.

It is doubtful whether foreign language has any place in the rural high school. If offered at all, it should be only in high schools strong enough to offer parallel courses for election, and should never displace the subjects lying closer to the interests and needs of the students.

The study of music and art begun in the elementary school should be continued in the high [Pg 91] school, and a love for the beautiful cultivated not only by the matter taught, but also by the æsthetic qualities of the school buildings and grounds and their decoration. On the practical sides these subjects will reach out to the beautifying of the farm homes and the life they shelter.

When a well-taught curriculum of some such scope of elementary and high school work as that suggested is as freely available to the farm child as his school is available to the city child, will the country boys and girls have a fair chance for education. And when this comes about, the greatest single obstacle to keeping our young people on the farm will have been removed.

FOOTNOTES:

[4] *Social Principles of Education,* p. 264.

IV

THE TEACHING OF THE RURAL SCHOOL

The importance of teaching

Teaching is the fundamental purpose for which the school is run. Taxes are levied and collected, buildings erected and equipped, and curriculum organized solely that teaching may go on. Children are clothed and fed and sent to school instead of being put at work in order that they may be taught. The school is classified into grades, programs are arranged, and regulations are enforced only to make teaching possible. Normal schools are established, teachers are trained, and certificates required in order that teaching may be more efficient.

The teacher confronts a great task. On the one hand are the children, ignorant, immature, and undeveloped. In them lie ready to be called forth all the powers and capacities that will characterize their fully ripened manhood and womanhood. Given the right stimulus and direction, these powers will grow into splendid strength and ca [Pg 93] pacity; lacking this stimulus and guidance, the powers are left crippled and incomplete.

On the other hand is the subject-matter of education, the heritage of culture which has been accumulating through the ages. In the slow process of human experience, running through countless generations, men have made their discoveries in the fields of mathematics and science; they have lived great events and achievements which have become history; they have developed the social institutions which we call the State, the church, the home, and the school; they have organized great industries and carried on complex vocations; they have crystallized their ideals, their hopes, and their aspirations in literature; and have with brush and chisel expressed in art their concepts of truth and beauty. The best of all this human experience we have collected in what we call a curriculum, and placed it before the child for him to master, as the generations before him have mastered it in their common lives. For only in this way can the child come into full possession of his powers, and set them at work in a fruitful way in accomplishing his own life-purpose.

It is the function of the teacher, therefore, to stand as an intermediary, as an interpreter, be [Pg 94] tween the child and this great mass of subject-matter that lies ready for him to learn. The race has lived its thousands or millions of years; the individual lives but a few score. What former generations took centuries to work out the child can spend only a few months or a few years upon. Hence he must waste no time and opportunity; he must make no false step in his learning, for he cannot in his short life retrieve his mistakes. It is the work of the teacher, through instruction and guidance, that is, through teaching, to save the child time in his learning and development, and to make sure that he does not lose his opportunity. And this is a great responsibility.

Thus the teacher confronts a problem that has two great factors, the *child* and the *subject-matter*. He must have a knowledge of both these factors if his work is to be effective; for he cannot teach matter that he does not know, and neither can he teach a person whose nature he does not understand. But in addition to a knowledge of these factors, the teacher must also master a technique of instruction, he must train himself in the art of teaching.

The teacher must know the child. It has been a rather common impression that if one knows a certain field of subject-matter, he will surely be [Pg 95] able to teach it to others. But nothing could be further from the truth than such an assumption. Indeed, it is proverbial that the great specialists are the most wretched teachers of their subjects. The nature of the child's mental powers, the order of their unfoldment, the evolution of his interests, the incentives that appeal to him, the danger points in both his intellectual and his moral development,—these and many other things about child nature the intelligent teacher must clearly understand.

And the teacher of the younger children needs this knowledge even more than the teacher of older ones. For the earlier years of the child's schooling are the most important years. It is at this time that he lays the foundation for all later learning, that he forms his habits of study and his attitude toward education, and that his life is given the bent for all its later development. Nothing can be more irrational, therefore, than to put the most untrained and inexperienced teachers in charge of the younger children. The fallacious notion that "anyone can teach little children" has borne tragic fruit in the stagnation and mediocrity of many lives whose powers were capable of great achievements.

The teacher must know the subject-matter. The [Pg 96] blind cannot successfully lead the blind. One whose grasp of a subject extends only to the simplest rudiments cannot teach these rudiments. He who has never himself explored a field can hardly guide others through that field; at least, progress through the field will be at the cost of great waste of time and failure to grasp the significance or beauty of what the field contains.

Expressed more concretely, it is impossible to transplant arithmetic, or geography, or history, or anything else that one would teach, immediately from the textbook into the mind of the child. The subject must first come to be very fully and completely a true possession of the teacher. The successful teacher must also know vastly more of a subject than he is required to teach. For only then has he freedom; only then has he outlook and perspective; only then can he teach the *subject*, and not some particular textbook; only then can he inspire others to effort and achievement through his own mastery and interest. Enthusiasm is *caught* and not taught.

The teacher must know the technique of instruction. For teaching is an art, based upon scientific principles and requiring practice to secure skill. One of the greatest tasks of the teacher is to *psychologize* the subject-matter for his pupils, [Pg 97] — that is, so to select, organize, and present it that the child's mind naturally and easily grasps and appropriates it. Teaching, when it has become an art, which is to say, when the teacher has become an artist, is one of the most highly skilled vocations. It is as much more difficult than medicine as the human mind is more baffling than the human body; it is as much more difficult than preaching as the child is harder to comprehend and guide than the adult; it is as much more difficult than the law as life is more complex than logic.

Yet, while we require the highest type of preparation for medicine, the ministry, or the law, we require but little for teaching. We pay enormous salaries to trained experts to apply the principles of scientific management to our industries or our business, but we have been satisfied with inexpert service for the teaching of our children. We are making fortunes out of the stoppage of waste in our factories, but allowing enormous waste to continue in our schools. *If we were to put into practice in teaching the thoroughly demonstrated and accepted scientific principles of education as we know them, we could beyond doubt double the educational results attained by our children.*

Teaching in the rural school

[Pg 98]

The criticisms just made on our standards of teaching will apply in some degree to all our schools from the kindergarten to the university; but they apply more strongly to the rural schools than to any other class. For the rural schools are the training-ground for young, inexperienced, and relatively unprepared teachers. Except for the comparatively small proportion of the town or city teachers who are normal school or college trained, nearly all have served an apprenticeship in the rural schools. Thus the rural school, besides its other handicaps, is called upon to train teachers for the more favored urban schools.

Careful statistical studies [5] have shown that many rural teachers, both men and women, have had no training beyond that of the elementary school. And not infrequently this training has taken place in the rural school of the type in which they themselves take up teaching. The average schooling of the men teaching in the rural schools of the entire country is less than two years above the elementary school, and of women, slightly more than two years. This is to say that our rural schools are taught by those who have had only about half of a high school course.

[Pg 99]

It is evident, therefore, that the rural teacher cannot meet the requirement urged above in the way of preparation. He does not know his subject-matter. Not only has he not gone far enough in his education to have a substantial foundation, breadth of view, and mental perspective, but he frequently lacks in the simplest rudiments of the immediate subject-matter which he is supposed to teach. The examination papers written by applicants for certificates to begin rural school teaching often betray a woful ignorance of the most fundamental knowledge. Inability to spell, punctuate, or effectively use the English language is common. The most elementary scientific truths are frequently unknown. A connected view of our nation's history and knowledge of current events are not always possessed. The great world of literature is too often a closed book. And not seldom the simple relations of arithmetical number are beyond the grasp of the applicant. In short, our rural schools, as they average, require no adequate preparation of the teacher, and do not represent as much education in their teaching force as that needed by the intelligent farmer, merchant, or tradesman. [Pg 100]

The rural teacher does not know the child. But little more than children themselves, and with little chance for observation or for experience in life, it would be strange if they did. They have had no opportunity for professional study, and psychology and the science of education are unknown to them. The attempts made to remedy this fatal weakness by the desultory reading of a volume or two in a voluntary reading-circle course do not serve the purpose. The teacher needs a thorough course of instruction in general and applied psychology, under the tutelage of an enthusiastic expert who not only knows his subject, but also understands the problems of the teacher.

The rural teacher does not know the technique of the schoolroom. The organizing of a school, the proper classification of pupils, the assignment of studies, the arrangement of a program of studies and recitation, the applications of suitable regulations and rules for the running of the school, are all matters requiring expert knowledge and skill. Yet the rural teacher has to undertake them without instruction in their principles and without supervisory guidance or help. No wonder that the rural school is poorly organized and managed. It presents problems of administration more puz [Pg 101] zling than the town school, and yet here is where we put out our novices, boys and girls not yet out of their "teens"—young people who themselves have no concept of the problems of the school, no knowledge of its complex machinery, and no experience to serve as a guide in confronting their work. No industrial enterprise could exist under such irrational conditions; and neither could the schools, except that mental waste and bankruptcy are harder to measure than economic.

Nor does the rural teacher know the technique of instruction any better than that of organization and management. The skillful conducting of a recitation is at least as severe a test upon mental resourcefulness and skill as making a speech, preaching a sermon, or conducting a lawsuit. For not only must the subject-matter be organized for immature minds unused to the formal processes of learning, but the effects of instruction upon the child's mind must constantly be watched by the teacher and interpreted with reference to further instruction. This skill cannot be attained empirically, by the cut-and-dried method, except at a frightful cost to the children. It is as if we were to turn a set of intelligent but untrained men loose in the community with their scalpels and their medicine cases to learn to be [Pg 102] surgeons and doctors by experimenting upon their fellows.

As would naturally be expected, therefore, the teaching in the average rural school is a dreary round of inefficiency. Handicapped to begin with by classes too small to be interesting, the rural teacher is mechanically hearing the recitations of some twenty-five to thirty of these classes per day. Lacking at the beginning the breadth of education that would make teaching easy, he finds it impossible to prepare for so many different exercises daily. The result is that the recitations are dull, spiritless, uninteresting. The lessons are poorly prepared by the pupils, poorly recited, and hence very imperfectly mastered. The more advanced work cannot stand on such a foundation of sand, and so, discouraged, the child soon drops out of school.

When it is also remembered that the tenure of service of the teacher is very short in the rural schools, the problem becomes all the more grave. The average term of service in the rural schools is probably not above two years, and in many States considerably below this amount. This requires that half of the rural teachers each year shall be beginners. It will be impossible, of course, as long as teaching is done so largely by girls, who nat [Pg 103] urally will, and should, soon quit teaching for marriage, to secure a long period of service in the vocation. Yet the rural school is, as we have seen, also constantly losing its trained teachers to the town and city, and hence breaking in more than its share of novices.

Added to the disadvantage inevitably coming from the brief period of service in teaching is a similar one growing out of a faulty method of administration. In a large majority of our rural schools the contract is made for but one term of not more than three months. This leaves the teacher free to accept another school at the end of the term, and not infrequently a school will have two or even three different teachers within the same year. There is a great source of waste at this point, owing to a change of methods, repetition of work, and the necessity of starting a new system of school machinery. Industrial concerns would hardly find it profitable to change superintendents and foremen several times a year. We do this in our schools only because we have not yet learned that it pays to apply rational business methods to education.

Nothing that has been said in criticism of rural teaching ought to be construed as a reflection on the rural teachers personally. The fact that [Pg 104] they can succeed as well as they do under conditions that are so adverse is the best warrant for their intelligence and devotion. It is not their fault that they begin teaching with inadequate knowledge of subject-matter, with ignorance of the nature of childhood, and without skill in the technique of the schoolroom. The system, and not the individual, is at fault. The public demands a pitifully low standard of efficiency in rural teaching, and the excellence of the product offered is not likely greatly to surpass what society asks and is ready to pay for.

Once again we must turn to the consolidated school as the solution of our difficulty. The isolated district school will not be able to demand and secure a worthy grade of preparation for teaching. The educational standards will not rise high enough under this system to create a public demand for skilled teachers. Nor can such salaries be paid as will encourage thorough and extensive study and preparation for teaching. And, finally, the professional incentives are not sufficiently strong in such schools to create a true craft spirit toward teaching.

While it is impossible to measure the improved results in teaching coming from the consolidated school in the same objective way that we can [Pg 105] measure increased attendance, yet there is no doubt that one of the strongest arguments for the consolidated school is its more skillful and inspiring teaching. The increased salaries, the possibility of professional association with other teachers, the improved equipment, the better supervision, and above all, the spirit of progress and enthusiasm in the school itself, all serve to transform teaching from a treadmill routine into a joyful opportunity for inspiration and service.

The training of rural teachers

The training of the rural teacher has never been given the same consideration as that of town or city teachers. It is true that normal schools are available to all alike, and that in a few States the rural schools secure a considerable number of teachers who have had some normal training. But this is the exception rather than the rule. In the Middle Western States, for example, where there is a rich agricultural population, whole counties can be found in which no rural teacher has ever had any special training for his work. Professional requirements have been on a par with the meager salaries paid, and other incentives have not been strong enough to insure adequate preparation. [Pg 106]

State normal schools have, therefore, been of comparatively little assistance in fitting teachers for the rural school. First of all the rural school teacher ordinarily does not go to the normal school, for it is not demanded of him. Again, if perchance a prospective rural teacher should attend a normal school, a town or city grade position is usually waiting for him when he graduates. For, in spite of the growth of our normal schools, they are as yet far from being able to supply all the teachers required for the urban grade positions, to say nothing about the rural schools. The colleges and universities are, of course, still further removed from the rural school, since the high schools stand ready to employ those of their graduates who enter upon teaching.

In some States, as for example, Wisconsin, county normal schools have been established with the special aim of preparing teachers for the rural schools. While this movement has helped, it does not promise to secure wide acceptance as a method of dealing with the problem. Greater possibilities undoubtedly exist in the comparatively recent movement toward combining normal training with the regular high school course. Provision for such courses now exists in New York, Pennsylvania, Ohio, Texas, Minnesota, [Pg 107] Iowa, Kansas, Nebraska, and a number of other States.

Combining normal training with high school education has first of all the advantage of bringing such training *to* prospective teachers, instead of requiring the teachers to leave home and incur additional expense in seeking their training. From the standpoint of the public it has the merit of economy, in that it utilizes buildings, equipment, and organization already in existence instead of requiring new.

But whatever may be the method employed, the rural teachers should receive better preparation for their work than they now have. This means, *first*, that the State must make adequate provision for the teacher to receive his training at a minimum of expense and trouble; and *second*, that the standard of requirement must be such that the teacher will be obliged to secure adequate preparation before being admitted to the school. Even with the present status of our rural schools it is not too much to require that every teacher shall have had *at least a four-year high school education*, and that *a reasonable amount of normal training* be had either in conjunction with the high school course, or subsequent to its completion. Indiana, for example, has found this [Pg 108] requirement entirely feasible, and a great influence in bettering the tone of the rural school.

Wherever the rural teacher secures his training, however, one condition must obtain: this preparation must familiarize him with the spirit and needs of the agricultural community, and imbue him with enthusiasm for service in this field. It is not infrequently the case that town high school graduates, themselves never having lived in the country, possess neither the sympathy nor the understanding necessary to enable them to offer a high grade of service in the rural school. Not a few of them feel above the work of such a position, and look with contempt or pity upon the life of the farm. The successful rural teacher must be able to identify himself very completely with the interests and activities of the community; nor can this be done in any half-hearted, sentimental, or professional manner. It must be a spontaneous and natural response arising from a true interest in the people, a knowledge of their lives, and a sincere desire for their welfare. Any preparation that does not result in this spirit, and train in the ability to realize it in action, does not fit for the rural school.

Salaries of rural teachers

[Pg 109]

The salaries paid teachers in general in different types of schools are one measure, though not a perfect one, of their efficiency. Salary is not a perfect measure of efficiency, (1) because economic ability to pay is a modifying influence. When the early New England teacher was receiving ten or twelve dollars a month and "boarding round," he was probably getting all that the community could afford to pay him, although he was often a college student, and not infrequently a well-trained graduate. The salaries paid in the various occupations are not (2) based upon any definite standards of the value of service. For example, the *chef* in a hotel may receive more than the superintendent of schools, and the football coach more than the college president; yet we would hardly want to conclude that the services of the cook and the athlete are worth more to society than the services of educators. And within the vocation of teaching itself there is (3) no fixed standard for judging teaching efficiency. Nevertheless, in general, teaching efficiency is in considerable degree measured by differences in salaries paid in different localities and in the various levels of school work. [Pg 110]

Based on the standard of salary as a measure, the teaching efficiency of rural teachers is, as we should expect from starting nearly all of our beginners here, considerably below that in towns or cities. A study by Coffman [6] of more than five thousand widely distributed teachers as to age, sex, salary, etc., shows that the average man in the rural school receives an annual salary of $390; in town schools, of $613; and in city schools, of $919. The average woman in the rural school receives an annual salary of $366; in town schools, of $492; and in city schools, of $591. Men in towns, therefore, receive one and one half times as much as men in the country, and in cities, two and one half times as much as in the country. Women in towns receive a little more than one and one third times as much as women in the country, and in the cities almost one and two thirds times as much as women in the country.

The actual amount of salary paid rural teachers is perhaps more instructive than the comparative amounts. The income of the rural teacher is barely a living wage, and not even that if the teacher has no parental home, or a gainful occupation during vacation times. Out of an [Pg 111] amount of less than four hundred dollars a year the teacher is expected to pay for a certificate, a few school journals and professional books, and attend teachers institutes or conventions, besides supporting himself as a teacher ought to live. It does not need argument to show that this meager salary forces a standard of living too low for efficiency. It would, therefore, be unfair to ask for efficiency with the present standard of salaries.

Nor is it to be overlooked that efficiency and salaries must mount upward together. It would be as unjust to ask for higher salaries without increasing the grade of efficiency as to ask for efficiency on the present salary basis. It is probable that the eighteen- or nineteen-year-old boys and girls starting in to teach the rural school, with but little preparation above the elementary grades, are receiving all they are worth, at least as compared with what they could earn in other lines. The great point of difficulty is that they are not worth enough. The community cannot afford to buy the kind of educational service they are qualified to offer; it would be a vastly better investment for the public to buy higher teaching efficiency at larger salaries. [Pg 112]

No statistics are available to show the exact percentage of increase in rural teachers' salaries during recent years, but this increase has been considerable; and the tendency is still upward. In this as in other features of the rural school problem, however, it will be impossible to meet reasonable demands without forsaking the rural district system for a more centralized system of consolidated schools. To pay adequate salaries to the number of teachers now required for the thousands of small rural schools would be too heavy a drain on our economic resources. Under the consolidated system a considerably smaller number of teachers is required, and these can receive higher salaries without greatly increasing the amount expended for teaching. In this as in other phases of our educational problems, what is needed is rational business method, and a willingness to devote a fair proportion of our wealth to the education of the young.

Supervision of rural teaching

Our rural school teaching has never had efficient supervision. The very nature of rural school organization has rendered expert supervision impossible, no matter how able the supervising officer might be. With slight modifications, the [Pg 113] office of *county superintendent* is, throughout the country, typical of the attempt to provide supervision for the rural school. While such a system may have afforded all that could be expected in the pioneer days, its inadequacy to meet present-day demands is almost too patent to require discussion.

First of all, it is physically impossible for a county superintendent to visit and supervise one hundred and fifty teachers at work in as many different schools scattered over four or five hundred square miles of territory. If he were to devote all his time to visiting country schools, he would have only one day to each school per year. When it is remembered that the county superintendent must also attend to an office that has a large amount of correspondence and clerical work, that he is usually commissioned with authority to oversee the building of all schoolhouses in his county, that he must act as judge in hearing appeals in school disputes, that he must conduct all teachers' examinations and in many instances grade the papers, and, finally, that country roads are often impassable, it is seen that his time for supervision is greatly curtailed. As a matter of fact some rural schools receive no visit from the county superintendent for several years at a time. [Pg 114]

A still further obstacle comes from the fact of the frequent changes of teachers among rural schools. A teacher visited by the county superintendent in a certain school this term, and advised as to how best to meet its problems, is likely to be in a different school next term, and required to meet an entirely new set of problems.

This is all very different from the problem of supervision met by the town or city superintendent. For the town or city district is of small area, and the schools few and close together. If the number of teachers is large, the superintendent is assisted by principals of different schools, and by deputies. The teaching force is better prepared, and hence requires less close supervision. School standards are higher, and the coöperation of patrons more easily secured. The course of study is better organized, the schools better graded and equipped, and all other conditions more favorable to efficient supervision. It would not, therefore, be just to compare the results of supervision in the country districts with those in urban schools without making full allowance for these fundamental differences.

The county superintendent is in many States discriminated against in salary as compared with other county officers, and, as a rule, no provision [Pg 115] is made to compensate for traveling expenses incurred in visiting schools. This, in effect, places a financial penalty on the work of supervision, as the superintendent can remain in his office with considerably less expense to himself than when he is out among the schools. In some instances, however, an allowance is made for traveling expenses in addition to the regular salary, thus encouraging the visiting of schools, or at least removing the handicap existing under the older system. An attempt has also been made in some States to relieve the county superintendent of the greater part of the clerical work of his office by employing for him at county expense a clerk for this purpose. These two provisions have proved of great help to the supervisory function of the county superintendent's work, but the task yet looms up in impossible magnitude.

The county superintendency is throughout the country almost universally a political office. In some States, as, for example, in Indiana, it is appointive by a non-partisan board. But, in general, the candidate of the prevailing party, or the one who is the best "mixer," secures the office regardless of qualifications. Sharing the fortunes of other political offices, the county superintendency frequently has applied to it the unwritten [Pg 116] party rule of "two terms and out," thus crippling the efficiency of the office by frequent changes of administration and uncertainty of tenure.

No fixed educational or professional standard of preparation for the county superintendency exists in the different States. If some reasonably high standard were required, it would do much to lessen the mischievous effects of making it a political office. In a large proportion of cases the county superintendent is only required to hold a middle-class certificate, and has enjoyed no better educational facilities than dozens of the teachers he is to supervise. The author has conducted teachers' institutes in the Middle West for county superintendents who had never attended an institute or taught a term of school. The salary and professional opportunities of the office are not sufficiently attractive to draw men from the better school positions; hence the great majority of county superintendents come from the village principalships, the grades of town schools, or even from the rural schools.

A marked tendency of recent years has been to elect women as county superintendents. In Iowa, for example, half of the present county superintendents are women, and the proportion is increasing. In not a few instances women have [Pg 117] made exceptional records as county superintendents, and, as a whole, are loyally devoted to their work. They suffer one disadvantage in this office, however, which is hard to overcome: they find it impossible, without undue exposure, to travel about the county during the cold and stormy weather of winter or when the roads are soaked with the spring rains. Whether they will be able to effect the desired coördination between the rural school and the agricultural interests of the community is a question yet to be settled.

In spite of the limitations of the office of county superintendent, however, it must not be thought that this office has played an unimportant part in our educational development. It has exerted a marked influence in the upbuilding of our schools, and accomplished this under the most unfavorable and discouraging circumstances. Among its occupants have been some of the most able and efficient men and women engaged in our school system. But the time has come in our educational advancement when the rural schools should have better supervision than they are now getting or can get under the present system.

The first step in improving the supervision, as in improving so many other features of the [Pg 118] rural schools, is the reorganization of the system through consolidation, and the consequent reduction in the number of schools to be supervised. The next step is to remove the supervising office as far as possible from "practical" politics by making it appointive by a non-partisan county board, who will be at liberty to go anywhere for a superintendent, who will be glad to pay a good salary, and who will seek to retain a superintendent in office as long as he is rendering acceptable service to the county. The third step is to raise the standard of fitness for the office so that the incumbent may be a true intellectual leader among the teachers and people of his county. Nor can this preparation be of the scholastic type alone, but must be of such character as to adapt its possessor to the spirit and ideals of an agricultural people.

A wholly efficient system of supervision of rural teaching, then, would be possible only in a system of consolidated schools, each under the immediate direction of a principal, himself thoroughly educated and especially qualified to carry on the work of a school adapted to rural needs. Over these schools would be the supervision of the county superintendent, who will stand in the same relation to the principals as that of the city [Pg 119] superintendent to his ward or high school principals. The county superintendent will serve to unify and correlate the work of the different consolidated schools, and to relate all to the life and work of the farm.

If it is said that systems of superintendence for rural schools could be devised more effective than the county superintendency, this may be granted as a matter of theory; but as a practical working program, there is no doubt that the office of county superintendent is a permanent part of our rural school system, unless the system itself is very radically changed. All the States, except the New England group, Ohio, and Nevada, now have the office of county superintendent. It is likely, therefore, that the plan of district superintendence permissive under the laws of certain States will hardly secure wide acceptance. The county as the unit of school administration is growing in favor, and will probably ultimately come to characterize the rural school system. The most natural step lying next ahead would, therefore, seem to be to make the conditions surrounding the office of county superintendent as favorable as possible, and then give the superintendent a sufficient number of deputies to make the supervision effective. These [Pg 120] deputies should be selected, of course, with reference to their fitness for supervising particular lines of teaching, such as primary, home economics, agriculture, etc. A beginning has already been made in the latter line by the employment in some counties, with the aid of the Federal Government, of an agricultural expert who not only instructs the farmers in their fields, but also correlates his work with the rural schools. This principle is capable of almost indefinite extension in our school system.

FOOTNOTES:

[5] See Coffman, *The Social Composition of the Teaching Force.*

[6] *The Social Composition of the Teaching Population.*

OUTLINE

I. THE RURAL SCHOOL AND ITS PROBLEM

- **The General Problem of the Rural School**

The Special Problem of the Rural School

- **The Adjustment of the Rural School to its Problem**

-

II. THE SOCIAL ORGANIZATION OF THE RURAL SCHOOL

The Rural School and the Community

The Consolidation of Rural Schools

Financial Support of the Rural School

The Rural School and its Pupils

III. THE CURRICULUM OF THE RURAL SCHOOL

The Scope of the Rural School Curriculum

The Rural Elementary School Curriculum

The Rural High School Curriculum

IV. THE TEACHING OF THE RURAL SCHOOL

The Importance of Teaching

• Teaching in the Rural School

The Training of Rural Teachers

Salaries of Rural Teachers

Supervision of Rural Teaching

[Pg 129]

RIVERSIDE EDUCATIONAL MONOGRAPHS

GENERAL EDUCATIONAL THEORY

- Dewey's MORAL PRINCIPLES IN EDUCATION.35
- Eliot's EDUCATION FOR EFFICIENCY.35
- Eliot's TENDENCY TO THE CONCRETE AND PRACTI-CAL IN MODERN EDUCATION .35
- Emerson's EDUCATION.35
- Fiske's THE MEANING OF INFANCY.35
- Hyde's THE TEACHER'S PHILOSOPHY.35
- Palmer's THE IDEAL TEACHER.35
- Prosser's THE TEACHER AND OLD AGE.60
- Terman's THE TEACHER'S HEALTH.60
- Thorndike's INDIVIDUALITY.35

ADMINISTRATION AND SUPERVISION OF SCHOOLS

- Betts's NEW IDEALS IN RURAL SCHOOLS.60
- Bloomfield's VOCATIONAL GUIDANCE OF YOUTH.60
- Cabot's VOLUNTEER HELP TO THE SCHOOLS.60
- Cole's INDUSTRIAL EDUCATION IN ELEMENTARY SCHOOLS.35
- Cubberley's CHANGING CONCEPTIONS OF EDUCA-TION.35
- Cubberley's THE IMPROVEMENT OF RURAL SCHOOLS.35
- Lewis's DEMOCRACY'S HIGH SCHOOL.60
- Perry's STATUS OF THE TEACHER.35
- Snedden's THE PROBLEM OF VOCATIONAL EDUCA-TION.35
- Trowbridge's THE HOME SCHOOL.60
- Weeks's THE PEOPLE'S SCHOOL.60

METHODS OF TEACHING

- Bailey's ART EDUCATION.60
- Betts's THE RECITATION.60
- Campagnac's THE TEACHING OF COMPOSITION.35
- Cooley's LANGUAGE TEACHING IN THE GRADES.35
- Dewey's INTEREST AND EFFORT IN EDUCATION.60
- Earhart's TEACHING CHILDREN TO STUDY.60
- Evans's TEACHING OF HIGH SCHOOL MATHEMAT-ICS.35
- Fairchild's THE TEACHING OF POETRY IN THE HIGH SCHOOL

- Haliburton and Smith's TEACHING POETRY IN THE GRADES.60
- Hartwell's THE TEACHING OF HISTORY.35
- Haynes's ECONOMICS IN THE SECONDARY SCHOOL.60
- Kilpatrick's THE MONTESSORI SYSTEM EXAMINED.35
- Palmer's ETHICAL AND MORAL INSTRUCTION IN THE SCHOOLS.35
- Palmer's SELF-CULTIVATION IN ENGLISH.35
- Suzzallo's THE TEACHING OF PRIMARY ARITHME-TIC.60
- Suzzallo's THE TEACHING OF SPELLING.60

[Pg 130]

RIVERSIDE TEXTBOOKS IN EDUCATION

Edited by Ellwood P. Cubberley, Head of the Department of Education, Leland Stanford, Jr., University.

The editor and the publishers have most carefully planned this series to meet the needs of students of education in colleges and universities, in normal schools, and in teachers' training courses in high schools. The books will also be equally well adapted to teachers' reading circles and to the wide-awake, professionally ambitious superintendent and teacher. Each book presented in the series will embody the results of the latest research, and will be at the same time both scientifically accurate, and simple, clear, and interesting in style.

The Riverside Textbooks in Education will eventually contain books on the following subjects: —

1. History of Education. — 2. Public Education in America. — 3. Theory of Education. — 4. Principles of Teaching. — 5. School and Class Management. — 6. School Hygiene. — 7. School Administration. — 8. Secondary Education. — 9. Educational Psychology. — 10. Educational Sociology. — 11. The Curriculum. — 12. Special Methods.

Now Ready

*RURAL LIFE AND EDUCATION.

By Ellwood P. Cubberley. $1.50 *net*. Postpaid. Illustrated.

*THE HYGIENE OF THE SCHOOL CHILD.

By Lewis M. Terman, Associate Professor of Education, Leland
Stanford Junior University. $1.65 *net*. Postpaid. Illustrated.

***THE EVOLUTION OF THE EDUCATIONAL IDEAL.**

By Mabel Irene Emerson, First Assistant in Charge,
George Bancroft
School, Boston. $1.00 *net*. Postpaid.

***HEALTH WORK IN THE SCHOOLS.**

By Ernest B. Hoag, Medical Director, Long Beach City
Schools,
California, and LEWIS M. TERMAN. Illustrated. $1.60
net.
Postpaid.

HOUGHTON MIFFLIN COMPANY
BOSTONNEW YORK CHICAGO

[Pg 131]

98

The HOUGHTON MIFFLIN PROFESSIONAL LIBRARY

For Teachers and Students of Education

THEORY AND PRINCIPLES OF EDUCATION

AMERICAN EDUCATION

By Andrew S. Draper, Commissioner of Education of the State of New
York. With an Introduction by Nicholas Murray Butler, President of
Columbia University. $2.00, *net*. Postpaid.

GROWTH AND EDUCATION

By John M. Tyler, Professor of Biology in Amherst College. $1.50,
net. Postpaid.

SOCIAL DEVELOPMENT AND EDUCATION

By M. Vincent O'Shea, Professor of Education in the University of
Wisconsin. $2.00, *net*. Postpaid.

THE PRINCIPLES OF EDUCATION

By William C. Ruediger, Ph. D., Assistant Professor of Educational
Psychology in the Teachers College of the George Washington
University. $1.25, *net*. Postpaid.

THE INDIVIDUAL IN THE MAKING

By Edwin A. Kirkpatrick, Teacher of Psychology, Child Study and
School Laws, State Normal School, Fitchburg, Mass.

$1.25, *net.*
Postpaid.

A THEORY OF MOTIVES, IDEALS, AND VALUES IN EDUCATION

By William E. Chancellor, Superintendent of Schools, Norwalk, Conn.
$1.75, *net.* Postpaid.

EDUCATION AND THE LARGER LIFE

By C. Hanford Henderson. $1.30, *net.* Postage 13 cents.

HOW TO STUDY AND TEACHING HOW TO STUDY

By Frank McMurry, Professor of Elementary Education in Teachers
College, Columbia University. $1.25, *net.* Postpaid.

[Pg 132]

The HOUGHTON MIFFLIN PROFESSIONAL LIBRARY

For Teachers and Students of Education

BEGINNINGS IN INDUSTRIAL EDUCATION

By Paul H. Hanus, Professor of the History and Art of Teaching in
Harvard University. $1.00, *net*. Postpaid.

PRACTICAL ASPECTS AND PROBLEMS

ETHICS FOR CHILDREN. A Guide for Teachers and Parents

By Ella Lyman Cabot, Member of the Massachusetts Board of
Education. $1.25, *net*. Postpaid.

CHARACTER BUILDING IN SCHOOL

By Jane Brownlee, formerly Principal of Lagrange School, Toledo,
Ohio. 16mo. $1.00, *net*. Postpaid.

HOW TO TELL STORIES TO CHILDREN

By Sara Cone Bryant. $1.00, *net*. Postpaid.

TALKS ON TEACHING LITERATURE

By Arlo Bates, Professor of English Literature in the Massachusetts
Institute of Technology. Professor Bates is also the author of
"Talks on the Study of Literature," "Talks on Writing English,"
etc. $1.30, *net*. Postpaid.

LITERATURE AND LIFE IN SCHOOL

By J. Rose Colby, Professor of Literature in the Illinois State
Normal University. $1.25, *net*. Postpaid.

THE KINDERGARTEN

By Susan Blow, Patty Hill, and Elizabeth Harrison, assisted by
other members of the Committee of Nineteen of the International
Kindergarten Union. With a Preface by Lucy Wheelock and an
Introduction by Annie Laws, Chairman of the Committee. 16mo. $1.25
net. Postpaid.